PLAYING

THROUGH THE

ABC'S

FAST, FREE AND FUN IDEAS TO INTRODUCE THE ALPHABET TO YOUR CHILD

BY CARLI SMITH

Playing through the ABC's by Carli Smith

©2020 Carli Smith

ISBN: 9780578768236

TABLE OF CONTENTS

WHAT IS THIS BOOK?

This book is filled with fast, easy, fun ways to introduce the alphabet to your child. One of the best parts about this book is that the activities require very little prep time and are mostly free! The activities in this book are simple and engaging ways to help your child understand that there are different letters of the alphabet, that each letter makes a different sound, and what those sounds are. There are so many different options to help teach children about the ABC's (workbooks, apps, games, videos on the internet, etc.), and I believe all of these are great ideas. BUT the ideas in this book provide something more than just learning the letters. These activities are simple ways for you to teach your child while spending time together, doing fun activities together, and making memories together. The activities in this book will help your child establish a love for learning and will allow you and your kiddo to have each other's full attention — even if it is just for ten minutes.

HOW TO USE THIS BOOK

When I started writing this book, I was already working on teaching my daughters the ABC's. I had three goals with helping my girls learn the alphabet, and I have those same three goals for this book. First, help children identify letters correctly. Second, understand that each letter makes a sound and know what those sounds are. Third, learn both of these things in a fun, engaging way that feels more like play than work.

Everyone might use this book a little differently and that's great! Some of you might have more time to do these activities with your child. Some children might already have a strong foundation of the alphabet, where this may be more of a review. Use this book however works best for you!

Here's how it works best for me and my daughters. I teach my girls one letter a week. I try to have at least three days that we learn about that letter during the week. On the first day we sing the ABC song together, and I introduce the new letter. We look at the letter (using the corresponding tear-out page at the back of the book), say the letter name, trace the letter with our fingers, and practice making the letter sound. I say the letter sound twice like this: "Ah. . Ah . . A" or if we are talking about an activity I'll say, "Ah . .Ah . .Ants. Ah . .Ah . .A. Ants start with the letter A." The best way to teach your kiddo the letter sound is repetition! For any new letter activity you do, try to repeat the letter you are learning about and what sound that letter makes at least twice. The more you repeat the letter sound and letter name together, the bigger impact this will have on your child. I follow the same pattern when making the letter sound and saying the letter name: **letter sound, letter sound, activity name; letter sound, letter sound, letter name.**

After we have said the letter name and sound several times, I pick an activity from the list for that letter. The activity I pick depends on how much time we have, if there are any materials needed, and if it's an inside or outside activity. We'll have fun doing the activity together, and I'll get my girls to say the letter name and sound as much as possible while doing the activity. When that activity is done, we might do another one or that might be it for the day. On the second and third day of learning, we review the letter sound, letter name, and what the letter looks like. I'll pick a few activities from the list for each day and maybe do an ambitious activity on the last day of learning about that letter. We also practice writing the letter and color a picture (that starts with that letter) using the pages at the back of this book. After we complete the coloring page for each letter, my girls help me three hole punch the paper and put it in their ABC binder. It's fun for them to look at all the work they have done and a great way to review all the letters we have learned about!

This is just one way to help teach your child the alphabet. There are lots of other great ways out there — videos, apps, workbooks, etc. I totally take advantage of these other ideas and my girls love using them! With kids it's great to mix it up and show them there are many different ways to learn. The advantage to taking the time to do the ideas listed in the rest of this book is they are very engaging activities that will get your kiddo excited about learning. These learning experiences also allow the two of you to spend time together bonding and having fun.

THINGS TO REMEMBER:

- Have your child say the letter name and sound as much as possible.

  (Letter sound, letter sound, activity name; letter sound, letter sound, letter name).

- Use the corresponding letter page (at the back of the book) to show your child what each letter looks like. Help them practice tracing and writing the letter.

- Pick and choose what activities work best for you and your kiddo.

- There are activities that work for every single letter on page 9. Use these activities as often as you want! We do the pillowcase surprise for almost every letter.

- Do these activities *with* your child! Don't just tell your kiddo to pretend to be an elephant — pretend to be an elephant with them (or whatever the activity is).

- Have fun! Be silly! Your attitude and energy are what makes the activities exciting for your little one.

- Be patient with your child — this is just an introduction to the ABC's.

- Be patient with yourself — if you go a few days (or even a few weeks) without teaching your kiddo a new letter, just pick back up when you can!

SAFETY FIRST

I t always amazes me how any item becomes dangerous when little kids are involved! I mean, we had an ER visit because of my daughter and a spoon once! All of the activities listed in this book are meant to be fun and engaging for your active little kiddo, but please keep safety in mind at all times. You know your child; you know what they can and cannot handle. If there is an activity that you don't think is a good idea for your child, do not do it. All of the activities have been safe and fine for my girls, but I understand every child is different. There are some activities that involve glue and/or scissors. If you don't feel like your kiddo is ready for these materials yet, don't do that activity. There are some activities that require the use of water. Do not leave your child unattended around water at any time, even for a second. Please use your best judgement to have fun and be safe.

ACTIVITIES THAT WORK FOR EVERY LETTER

In the next several pages there are specific activities listed for each letter. Some letters have just a few activities (X, Y and Z are hard, people!) while some letters have tons of ideas! Below are ideas that will work for every single letter. You can use them as often as you want! My girls could do the hide and seek letter activity all day, every day (which is great because that's an easy one for me to get ready).

- **Trace the letter with your finger.** Each letter has its own tear-out page at the back of this book. Find the letter you are working on that day and practice tracing both the capital and lower-case letter together.

- **Practice writing the letter.** Each tear-out page also has space to practice writing the capital and lower-case of each letter; do this with your child. Some children might be able to trace the letter independently, and some might need you to help them hold the crayon (or pencil). After you have used the writing space on the tear-out sheet you can use any piece of paper to practice even more. There are also several blank pages at the very back of this book that you can use for extra practice. You can even put the tear-out page into a clear, protective sheet and use an expo marker to practice tracing and writing the letter over and over. My daughter really enjoys practicing writing the letters on a small Etch-a-Sketch.

- **Paint the letter.** My girls and I both love this form of "painting" (I love it because it doesn't require much clean up). Get different colors of construction paper and, using a marker, write the letter you are learning about on one of the colored papers. Then, fill a small container with water and get a paintbrush. If you don't have a paintbrush, use a Q-tip or your fingers (my girls end up using their fingers even when we do have paintbrushes). Dip the paintbrush into the water and trace the letter. The colored construction paper will turn a darker shade of that color and your kiddo will be able to see their tracing work. My two-year-old just likes watching how the paper turns a darker color, but my three-year-old actually does pretty well at tracing the letter and even forming the letter by herself!

- **Look up videos/images for that letter.** I hate to admit it, but my girls love the TV and iPad. They both love watching movies, songs and playing games on my iPad. Many of the activities in this book are focused on getting away from the TV, but I justify that this activity is fine as long as I'm spending time with my girls and doing this *with* them (not just turning on the TV and walking away). On some of the days we are talking about a letter, I will grab my iPad (or use my phone) and we'll look up songs and movies about the letter we are learning about. I'll also think of different items that start with that letter and look up images or short movies of this to show my girls. You can look up foods, animals, places, instruments, people, things in nature — honestly, anything you can think of that starts with that letter!

- **Letter Hide-and-Seek.** This activity requires paper, something to write with, and possibly scissors. Cut (or tear) your paper into a few pieces. I usually do 4–6 pieces. If I'm lucky and can find sticky notes in the junk drawer, I'll just use those. Write the letter you are learning about onto each piece of paper. Instruct your kiddo to go into a different room and quickly hide the pieces of paper. I tell my girls to practice singing the ABC's or count to 10 while I hurry and hide all the papers. When all the papers are hidden, have your child come back into the room and watch them excitedly search for each letter!

  - If you are trying to do this activity with a bigger group of kids, you have options. You can hide one letter paper for each kiddo. Instruct each child that once they have found one letter, they need to sit down and watch other children find their paper. You can also have one or two kids go into a different room (these would be your "seekers") and have the rest of the kids help you hide the letter papers. The "hiders" can raise their hands and give you an idea of where to hide a paper or even hide the papers themselves.

● **Pillowcase Surprise.** This activity does require materials and a few minutes of prep time. Find items around your house that start with the letter you are learning about. Collect these items and put them into a pillowcase (or bag). Have your kiddo pull out one item at a time and talk about that item. For every item, make sure you are helping your child make the connection to the letter you are learning about that day. For example, we might be discussing the letter "B" and my daughter would pull a book out of the pillowcase. We would practice saying, "Buh . . Buh . . .B. Buh . . .Buh. . .Book. Book starts with the letter B". And then go on to read the book together.

SEASONAL IDEAS AND AMBITIOUS ACTIVITIES

This book contains quite a few activities for each letter, but there will always be more ideas and activities to add for each letter. A fun way to add more activities and make the activities even more relevant to your child is by taking into consideration the seasons, weather, holidays and people in your lives. For example, when learning about the letter "R" with my girls I put a picture of my daughter (Remi) in for the pillowcase surprise activity. When the picture was pulled out we practiced saying, "Rrr . . .Rrr . . . Remi. Rrr . . . Rrr . . .R. Remi starts with the letter R." Try to incorporate your child's name and the names of family members or close friends when possible. I also take the weather into consideration and see if there's any outside activities we can do that work with the letter we are learning about. Here are some ideas:

- **Weather.** Look outside and see if you can use the weather to talk about today's letter. For example, if it's raining you could use that to discuss many different letters! R–rain, C–cloudy, G–gray skies, W–wet ground, U–umbrella, P–puddles, etc. If there's no lightning and you have time, you can go outside and play in the rain or simply put a cup outside and see how full the cup gets by the time it finishes raining. If it's sunny and hot outside, you could discuss S–sunny, H–hot, B–blue skies, C–clouds, W–windy, etc. Get creative and see what letters you can discuss to get you and your little one outside.

- **Seasons.** Winter, Spring, Summer, and Fall. You can talk about the season and the things that come with it — the weather, specific holidays, changes in nature at that time of year, etc. Right now, it's summer so if my girls and I were learning about the letter "S", we would talk about **summer**, go outside and feel the heat from the **sun**, and possibly go **swimming.** If it was winter and we were learning about the letter "C", we would talk about it getting **colder** outside, different **clothes** we wear in winter (hats, mittens, coats, etc.), and hot **cocoa.** I would bundle my girls up in the winter clothes we talked about, go outside and play in the cold, and come back in for some cocoa. With all of these activities, remember to mention the letter and letter sound you are learning about as much as possible (Sss . . . Sss . . . Summer. Sss . . .Sss . . . Swimming. Sss. . . Sss. . . S).

- **Holidays.** I LOVE celebrating holidays and birthdays! Even when we're on a tight budget, I try to make the holidays special and do something unique for that day. If there's a holiday or birthday coming up, think about how you can incorporate it into your alphabet learning fun. For example, if Valentine's day was coming soon, I would get creative about how to include this in our letter learning activities. Here are some ideas for that holiday:

H – Heart, draw hearts together

L – Love, talk about things and people you love

C – Color a Valentine's card

S – Snack, make a special Valentine's snack (like heart shaped cookies)

F – Flowers, bring flowers to someone special

You can do this for any holiday! I'm not sure why, but incorporating holiday activities makes planning these learning activities more fun for me. My girls always seem to get extra excited about holiday projects as well.

- **Ambitious Activities.** My goal for this book was to come up with easy, inexpensive activities for each letter that you and your child would enjoy doing together. I wanted you to be able to pick up the book, scan through the activities and immediately be able to do an activity with no prep need-ed. There are obviously more activities that you could come up with for each letter, but some activities might require more time, energy, materials, or money. I have listed a few "ambitious" activities if you're looking for an extra special learning activity. The ambitious activities usually require a few materials, might take more time, or require you to go somewhere. I do not put pressure on myself to do an ambitious activity for every letter. We do these special learning experiences when the activity is convenient for us and when we have more time to do letter learning activities that day.

"A" can make two sounds — a long sound and a short sound. The long sound is when "A" says its name, like in the word "acorn". The short sound is when "A" makes the "ah" sound, like in the word "apple".

- Go on an **Ant** Hunt **Adventure**
  - Take your little one outside and look for ants together.
- Munch on **Apples**
  - Try a few different apples and see which ones you like the best!
- Look up pictures of **Alligators**
- Pretend to be **Astronauts**
  - Put on your pretend helmets and tell each other what you see in space!
- **Artwork** — drawing, stamps, painting, stickers, coloring, etc.
- Draw pictures of **Aliens** — make them as crazy looking as you can!
- Make paper **Airplanes** or go outside and watch for airplanes in the sky.
- Help your kiddo locate their **Arms**, **Armpits** and **Ankles**
- **Arm** exercises
  - Wiggle and stretch your arms, do big and little circles with your arms, lift items to get strong muscles in your arms (we lift stuffed animals and pillows).
- Sing the **ABC** song

- **Animals**
  - Pretend to be different animals, talk about your favorite animals, go on a walk and see what animals you can find.

- Make an **Angry** face
  - Talk about good ways to cope with being angry such as counting to 10, taking deep breaths, or walking away and having time to yourself.

Seasonal Activity: Autumn

If you happen to start this book in Autumn, explain to your child that Autumn is a season during the year when the leaves change colors and fall off the trees and the weather starts to get cold. Go outside and point out the leaves changing colors on the trees and collect any leaves that have fallen on the ground. You can even bring the leaves inside and glue them onto a paper for an Autumn leaf collage! If you live somewhere that is warm all year, draw (or trace) leaves onto a piece of paper and color them fall colors (red, yellow and orange). If you prefer "Fall" to "Autumn" you can do this same activity when you get to the letter "F".

Bb

- Go outside and listen for **Birds**
  - It's crazy how quiet kids get for activities like this!

- **Blow Bubbles**
  - If you don't have any bubbles, you can plug a sink or bathtub and help your kiddo make bubbles with dish or hand soap.

- **Bear** Hunt song/ **Baby** Shark song
  - Look up Bear Hunt and/or Baby Shark songs to dance and sing to together.

- Go outside on a **Bug** Hunt Adventure

- Draw pictures of **Butterflies** and **Bumblebees**

- Make the **Bed**

- Snuggle in a **Blanket** and read a **Book**

- Locate **"B"** foods in the kitchen
  - Beans, bread, bacon, bananas, butter, blueberries, etc.

- Identify items that are **Blue, Brown & Black**
  - It's easier to stay in one room (such as your child's bedroom) and help them locate all the items.

- **Bounce Balls**, play **Basketball**, roll a **Ball**, etc.

- **Band-Aids**
  - My girls want band-aids ALL the time, for no good reason! Let your child pick out a band-aid to wear just because.

- Hop like a **Bunny**

- Ride **Bikes**

- Sing the children's song, "The Wheels on the **Bus**"

- **Blanket** Ride
  - Have your child *lie* on a blanket and pull them around on it. Be careful with this one! If your child sits on the blanket and you pull too fast, they will fall backwards and hit their head. I have found it's a lot safer to only do this activity when my girls are lying down on the blanket.

- **Bubble** Gum
  - I don't let my munchkins have gum yet, but they LOVE when I blow bubbles (with my gum) and take turns popping the bubbles.

Ambitious Activities.

Bake Brownies.

Build Something. You can make this as simple or as complex as you want! You can make a tent out of blankets and pillows. You could build a castle using toy blocks or build a house for a stuffed animal using whatever materials you have around the house.

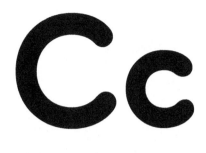

Cc

The letter "C" can make a "k" sound as well as a "s" sound. At this early stage of learning it's best to focus on the "k" sound.

- **Color** a picture
- Go on a walk and try to find a **Cat**
  - Don't feel like going outside? Pretend to be cats in the living room!
- Locate **"C"** food items in the kitchen
  - Carrots, crackers, corn, coffee, etc.
- Draw pictures of **Cupcakes** and **Cookies**
- Practice **Cutting** skills
  - Draw a few lines on a piece of paper and help guide your child to cut down the line. This requires A LOT of patience, but your child's future teacher will thank you!
- **Clap** your hands
  - Loud, quiet, fast, slow, high, low, behind your back, etc.
- **Clean** something
  - This can be as simple as pretending to clean a dirty toy or as complex as cleaning your child's room together.
- Feel the **Cold**
  - Grab an item from the fridge/freezer and let your kiddo feel how cold it is.
- Practice **Counting**
  - Think of a few easy items to count together (fingers, toys, doors in the house, etc.).

- **Crunch** on a loud snack together
  - This is the only time I ever encourage my kids to chew loud enough so I can hear them, and they love it!

- Pretend to have a **Camera**
  - It's fun to see what your child wants to take pictures of. Make sure to say "Click!" when you snap your pics!
  - If possible, let your child use your phone to take pictures. When you are done, take time to look through the pictures together.

- **Comb** each other's hair

- Pretend to be a **Cow**

- Look up pictures of **Clowns** — Not the creepy ones!

- **Call** someone — Or simply pretend to.

- **Crawl** on the ground

- Build a **Cup Castle**
  - We use plastic, throw away cups for this activity.

Ambitious Activities.

Bake Cookies or Cupcakes.

Let your child pick out a Craft from the store and do the craft together.

Weather: Cold

If it happens to be a cold day outside when you are learning about the letter "C", you can bundle up and go on a short walk to feel the cold. If you aren't up to going on a cold walk, you can open a door or window for a few minutes and still feel the cold.

Weather: Cloudy

If there are clouds outside, look at the clouds together. Use your imagination and take turns telling each other what the clouds resemble.

Holiday: Christmas

If your family celebrates Christmas and it's Christmas time, you can incorporate that into learning about the letter "C". You can sing Christmas songs, get out Christmas decorations, make holiday Cookies, watch a Christmas movie, etc.

Dd

- **DANCE!**
    - The only time I ever even attempt to dance is if it's just me and my girls at home (with all the blinds down).

- Look up pictures of **Dinosaurs/Dolphins**

- Go on a walk and hope to see (or hear) a **Dog**

- Draw pictures of **Donuts**

- Pretend to be a **Dentist** or **Doctor**
    - My girls love pretending their stuffed animals are "sick" and we have to make them feel better.

- Get a **Drink** together

- Pretend to **Drive**
    - Act out all the steps together — climbing in the car seat, buckling up, putting keys in, turning on music, pushing the gas pedal and stopping. You can also grab a plate and pretend it's the steering wheel to turn and honk.

- **Door** — knock on the door, locate and count all the doors in the house.

- Play a **Drum**
    - We pretend that a pot turned upside down is our drum and make different beats.

- Pretend to be a **Duck**
    - Yes, this includes waddling and quacking!

- Practice writing "**D**" in the **Dirt**.
  - **Dig** in the **Dirt**

- **Dice** — roll the dice and practice counting the **Dots.**

Ambitious Activity.

If you live close to an area with ducks, go on an outing to feed the ducks.

Ee

The letter "E" can make several different sounds. The long sound is when "E" says its name, as in the word "eat". The short sound is when "E" makes the "eh" sound, like in the word "egg".

- Locate your **Ears**, **Eyes** & **Elbows**

- **Eye** contest — stare into each other's eyes and try not to blink

- Pretend to be **Elephants**

- Look up pictures of **Eels**

- Crack an **Egg** open and talk about it

- Draw a picture of the **Earth**

- **Exercise** together
    - This could be going on a short walk or doing a few different work-out activities inside.

- **Eat** something yummy

- Use an **Eraser**
    - I'm embarrassed to admit my girls never used an eraser before this activity! We made small doodles on a paper (using a pencil) and then practiced erasing them.

- **Explore** somewhere new!
    - Try out a new park or playground, go on a different walking route, check out a store you haven't been in before, etc.

Ambitious Activity.

Eggs. Show your kiddo that there are several different ways to cook eggs. Teach them that when you cook eggs differently, the end results look different. For example, you can scramble an egg and cook an egg over easy and talk about the differences with your child. If you aren't a fan of eating plain eggs like this (or stinking up your kitchen with egg smell), you can also make something that calls for eggs in the recipe.

Ff

- Go outside and look for **Flowers**
  - You can also draw or paint pictures of flowers.

- Locate your **Face**, **Fingers** and **Feet**
  - Play "This little Piggy" on your child's feet

- **Feel** different textures (hard, soft, smooth, rough, etc.)

- Ask your kiddo "**Favorite**" questions
  - What's your favorite color? Food? Drink? Toy? Etc.

- Do something **FUN!**
  - Do an activity together that you know your child loves.

- **Food** — make or eat something yummy together

- Draw a picture of your **Family**

- Count your **Fingers**

- Trace your **Feet**

- Pretend to be **Frogs**
  - This includes jumping and ribbeting!

- **Funny Faces**
  - Make funny faces in front of the mirror (or take pictures on your phone).

- Look up pictures of **Fish**
  - There are some crazy looking fish out there!

- Pretend to **Fly**

- **Flashlight**
  - Go into a dark room and turn on a flashlight. If you don't have a flashlight you can use the light from your phone.

- Make a **Fan**
  - Color a piece of paper, fold it back and forth (accordion style), hold the bottom of the paper tight together, and spread out the top part.

- Locate **Fruit** in the kitchen

Holiday: Fourth of July

If you happen to be learning about the letter "F" close to the fourth of July, you can incorporate this holiday into a letter activity! Draw pictures of fireworks and then watch fireworks once it gets dark with your little one. You can also color a paper to look like the American flag and help your kiddo color one as well!

Gg

- Look up pictures of **Gorillas** and **Giraffes**

- Air **Guitar**
  - Turn up some old school Rock 'n Roll and teach your munchkin how to rock out on that air guitar of theirs!

- Go outside and look for **Grasshoppers**

- Walk barefoot in the **Grass**

- Pretend to be spooky **Ghosts**

- Locate items that are **Green**
  - This is a good color to look for outside.

- Play a **Game** together

- Draw a picture of a **Gingerbread** man
  - My girls love saying this anytime we talk about gingerbread: "Run, run, run, as fast as you can! You can't catch me! I'm the Gingerbread man!"

- Go on a walk and locate **Gates**

- Make **Goat** noises

- Eat **Goldfish** (crackers)

- **Garbage** — have your kiddo help you take the garbage out.

- Call **Grandparents** (or look at pictures of them)

- **Growing** up
  - Talk about growing up and getting big! Measure how tall your child is and see how much they weigh. This is great practice for doctor visits!

Ambitious Activities.

Practice Gluing skills. I know — it's sticky and messy and kind of a pain to do, BUT kids need to practice this skill, and most kids love using glue! This activity can be as simple as ripping up pieces of paper and gluing those pieces onto a bigger paper.

Give a Gift. You can make this as simple as you want! Your child can color a picture and give it to someone. You can make cookies together for a neighbor. You could let your kiddo pick out a treat from the store and surprise a sibling with it.

Hh

- Pretend to be **Horses**

- Locate your **Hair**, **Hand**, **Heart** and **Head**

- Sing the **Happy** song
    - "If you're Happy and you know it clap your hands . . .stomp your feet . . . blink your eyes . . ." etc.

- Go on a walk and look at different **Houses**

- Give a **Hug**

- Do **High-Fives**

- Sing the children's song, "**Head**, shoulders, knees and toes"

- Pretend to fix something with a **Hammer**
    - If you don't want your kiddo to have a hammer, use an object that resembles a hammer or just pretend.

- Look up pictures of **Hippos**

- Wear a **Hat** or do silly **Hair**

- Play **Hide** and Seek
    - If you don't want to actually go around the house hiding, have your child pick out an item and take turns hiding and finding it in one room of your house.

- **Howl** like a wolf

- Say "**Hello**" to everyone you see on a walk

- Draw a picture of your **Home**
- Practice **Hanging** shirts on a **Hanger**
- Trace your **Hands**

Ambitious Activity.

Teach your munchkin how to play Hop Scotch.

Weather: Hot

If it's hot outside when you're learning about the letter "H", go outside and talk about the change in temperature from being inside. You can put an ice cube on the ground and watch the heat melt it or eat popsicles together.

Holiday: Halloween

If your family celebrates Halloween and you're learning about the letter "H" around Halloween time, bring this into your learning activities! You can see what items you have around the house to create home-made costumes (this can be as simple as throwing a light blanket over your head and pretending to be a spooky ghost). You can also go to a pumpkin patch (or your local grocery store) and pick out pumpkins. If you don't feel up to carving them, you can always paint or color the pumpkins!

Another tricky vowel! The long "I" sound says its name, like in the word "ice". The short sound is when "I" sounds more like "ih", as in the word "iguana".

- **Ice** Cube
  - Put an ice cube in a plastic bag and let your child play with it and feel the cold.

- Draw **Ice Cream** pictures

- Play "**I-Spy**"

- Look up pictures of **Iguanas**

- Show your child what an **Igloo** is
  - You can draw a picture or look this up.

- Practice using the word "**I**"
  - *I* am three years old. *I* am happy/sad. *I* am a boy/girl. Etc.

- **Inside**
  - Show the difference between inside and outside. This can be walking in and outside several times or showing the difference by a window ("The bird is outside. We are inside").

- **In**
  - Place a small object in something to show what "in" means. The book is *in* the drawer. The teddy bear is *in* the bed. The food is *in* the fridge. Etc.

- Pretend to play different **Instruments**
  - Or look up instruments and the noises they make online.

- Sing the children's song, "**Itsy** Bitsy Spider"

- Go outside and look for **Insects**
  - If it's too cold or you'd rather stay inside, look up pictures of insects.

Ambitious Activity.

Make Ice Cream! There are a lot of simple ice cream recipes online. If this seems a little too ambitious and you have an extra dollar or two, you can go out for ice cream together!

- **JUMP!**
    - High, low, fast, slow, loud, quiet, one foot, both feet, etc.
- **Jog**
    - Either outside or jogging in place works too!
- Help your kiddo practice putting on a **Jacket**
- Throw **Junk** in the garbage
    - You might have to "find" some junk before-hand for this activity.
- Make and drink **Juice** together
- Try to **Juggle**
- Look up pictures of **Jellyfish**
- Do **Jumping Jacks**
- Pretend to be a **Jack**-in-the-Box toy
    - We do this by crouching down low, putting our hands in front of us and pretending to crank a handle with one hand. When I yell "Jack in the Box" we all jump up as high as we can!
- **Jello**
    - Make it, eat it, play with it, squish it, etc. If you don't have time to make the jello, grab the pre-made kind from your local grocery store.
- Sing "**Jingle** Bells"
- **Jungle**
    - Show your child pictures of the jungle and talk about what you might see there. Draw your own picture of the jungle.

- **Jar**
  - Find a jar and let your kiddo fill it with something (water, grass, rocks, cotton balls, small toys, etc.).

> **Ambitious Activity.**
>
> I'm playing off of the Junk option listed above. If you wanted to take this a step further, you can use this as an opportunity to go through toys, books, stuffed animals and get rid of the "junk". Have your child help you decide which toys are worth keeping and which ones can be donated or thrown out. (Whenever I try this we end up throwing out about 2 small toys — but that's 2 less toys to pick up around the house.)

Kk

- Be **Kind**
  - Talk about what "kind" means and come up with something kind you can do for someone else. This can be as simple or as complex as you want it to be. An example of being kind can be helping mom clean up the mess of toys on the floor.

- **Kick** a ball
  - I take my girls to the park quite a bit, but we don't normally kick balls into the soccer goal. They loved doing this, and it was fun to mix it up at the park!
  - If you would rather stay inside and don't want to destroy your house, pretend to kick.

- Blow a **Kiss**
  - Put chapstick or lipstick on your little one and have them "kiss" a piece of paper (so they can see their "kiss").

- Show off your **Karate** moves

- Hop like a **Kangaroo**

- Meow like a **Kitten**

- Show your kiddo how **Keys** work
  - This can be house keys or car keys. If you don't have any keys available, look up pictures of keys and explain that keys help us open things.

- Look up pictures of **Koalas**

- Pretend to be a **King**

- Take a tour around your **Kitchen**.
    - Have your child name items that you point to and show them a few items in the kitchen that might be new to them. You can show them something "cool" — like how the can opener or cheese grater works.

Ambitious Activity.

Make a Kite! Cut a piece of paper into a big diamond (so it looks like a kite) and let your little one color it. When they are done, tape a piece of string/yarn/dental floss (whatever you can find in your house!) to the diamond and you have a kite.

Ll

- **Love**
    - Draw a heart and talk about people and things that you love.

- **Lick** something
    - . . . preferably something edible . . .
    - If you have lemons or limes these are fun ones to try and they start with the letter "L".

- Pretend to be **Lions**

- Turn the **Lights** on and off

- **Lids**
    - Find a few items that have lids and have your child practice taking the lids on and off. Easy items might be plastic containers, small boxes, empty water bottles, etc.

- Look up pictures of **Lobsters**

- Pretend to climb up a **Ladder**

- Go outside and collect **Leaves**

- Locate **Legs** and **Lips**

- Draw a picture of a **Ladybug**

- Play Follow the **Leader**; take turns being the leader.

- Be **Loud**! Sing a song or count to 10 as loud as you can.

- **Laundry**
    - Have your kiddo help you put dirty clothes in the washer and let them push the buttons to start it up.

- **Laugh** together
  - Tickle your little one or watch a silly video together. My girls get laughing the loudest when I chase them and tickle them when I catch them!

- **Lines**
  - Help your child practice drawing straight lines on a piece of paper. You can also gather up small items and have your child line the items up.

Ambitious Activities.

Take a trip to the Library.

Large and Little. Gather quite a few objects of different sizes from around your house. Help your kiddo categorize each item as "large" or "little".

Mm

- **Make** something!
  - Make a snack, make a tower, make up a game, etc.

- **Mirror** Time
  - Look into the mirror together and make different faces (happy, mad, sad, scared, surprised, silly, etc.).

- **Mail**
  - Write a letter (or color a picture) and show your child how to mail it to someone.
  - Go on a walk and locate the **Mailbox**.

- **Money**
  - Show your kiddo what money looks like (or a credit card if you don't have cash/coins). Explain that we use money to buy things and talk about fun things to buy (food, treats, books, toys, etc.). If you happen to have coins, help your toddler group the same coins together.

- Turn on some **Music** (and dance)!

- Pretend to be **Monkeys**

- Look up pictures of the **Moon**
  - Look at the Moon outside if it's nighttime.

- Drink **Milk** — Pretending to drink milk works too!

- Draw a **Map** together
  - It can be a map from your front door to your child's bedroom, a map of your neighborhood, a treasure map, etc.

- Pretend to **Mix** something
  - Mix fast and slow, ask your munchkin what food they are "making".

Ambitious Activities.

Practice Matching! Socks are an easy item to use for this activity. Get several different pairs of socks (make sure each one has a match) and put them in a pile on the floor. Explain to your child that you are going to put together the socks that look the same. You might need to match a pair or two together at first to *show* them what matching looks like.

Be a Mummy! Get a roll of toilet paper and wrap your little one up like a mummy. Make sure to do this close to a mirror or take a picture on your phone so your kiddo can see what they look like as a mummy. If your child doesn't want to be completely wrapped like a mummy, do mummy legs or mummy arms!

Nn

- Pretend to take a **Nap**
    - You can also get stuffed animals and blankets and help all the stuffed animals take a nap.
- Make silly **Noises**
- **Numbers**
    - Write down the numbers 1–10 and practice counting out loud while you both point to the correct number.
- Locate your **Nose**, **Neck** and **Nails**
    - Paint your Nails
- Look up a picture of a **Net**
    - Talk about different things you can catch in a Net.
- Go on a walk around the **Neighborhood**
    - See if you can find a bird **Nest** on your walk!
- Help your child write their **Name**
- Be **Nice**
    - Do something nice for someone else.
    - Practice talking nice (please, no thank you, excuse me, etc.).
- Ask Yes/**No** questions
    - "Do you like broccoli?" "Do you like snakes?" Etc. Ask questions that you're pretty sure they'll respond to with a "no".
- **Night**
    - Turn off the lights and pretend it's night-time. Have your child help you walk through your night-time routine. For us that looks like going to the bathroom, putting on pajamas, brushing our teeth, reading a book and getting tucked in.

Ambitious Activity.

Cook Noodles and play with them together! Let your kiddo feel and squish them (once they have cooled down!). You can even cook a few different kinds of noodles and talk about the differences. If you're feeling extra ambitious, let your little one play chef and add sauces and spices to their noodles. My girls usually add some crazy things to their noodles, so we don't actually eat these noodles after.

Holiday: New Years

If you happen to be learning about the letter "N" close to January, you can talk about New Years with your kiddo! Write down what year it is going to be in big numbers and help your child identify each individual number. For example, if it is going to be 2021, I would help my girls identify 2, 0, 2 and 1.

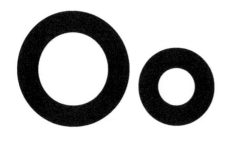

"O" has a long sound and a short sound. Long "O" sounds like "oh" as in the word "open". Short "O" sounds like "awe" as in the word "octopus".

- Play **Outside**!
- Locate items that are **Orange**
- Eat an **Orange**
- Look up pictures of **Octopi**
- **Open** doors, drawers and cupboards
    - If this seems too loud or annoying, have your munchkin practice opening books or opening a box.
- Make an **Obstacle** course
    - Throw items on the floor to hop over, crawl over, run around, stomp on, etc.
- Hoot like an **Owl**
- **Oink** like a Pig
- **On/Off**
    - Practice turning something on and off. My girls really like turning the sink water and bathroom lights on and off.
- Locate the **Oven**
    - Talk about oven safety and foods you can cook in the oven.
- Look at pictures of the **Ocean**
    - Talk about things you might see in the ocean. Draw an ocean picture together.

Ambitious Activity.

Make Oatmeal. I'm not a fan of regular oatmeal, so we make silly oatmeal! We do this by mixing together oats and water, then adding whatever spices and sauces we want to it!

- Locate items that are **Pink** & **Purple**
  - Remember to do this *with* your child.
- **Paint**
  - One of the easiest ways to have your kiddo "paint" is to get water, a paint brush, and different colored construction paper. Simply dip the paint brush in the water, brush the water onto the paper, and watch the construction paper turn a darker shade of that color.
    - No paint brush? Use Q-tips.
    - No Q-tips? Use your fingers.
- Go outside and **Point** to different things
  - Point to trees, the sky, grass, your house, etc.
- Draw a **Picture**
- **Play** at the **Park/Playground**
  - Or Play a game inside that your child loves.
- **Pop** some **Popcorn**
- **Pretend**
  - Pretend to be different animals, pretend to be somewhere else (like the grocery store), pretend to be someone else (like a doctor, princess or chef).
- Look at **Pictures**
  - This could be pictures on your phone, pictures around your house, or a picture album.

- Find **Pockets**
  - Try to find items of clothing that have pockets. My girls and I do this one in the laundry room as I'm throwing another load of wash in!

- Look up a video of someone playing the **Piano**

- Attempt to do **Push-ups**

- Pretend to be a **Pig**

- Write with a **Pen**
  - I very rarely have my girls write/color with a pen, so even though this is a simple activity, they love it!

- Make your own **Puzzle**
  - Color a picture, cut the picture into pieces (I usually cut the paper into 6 pieces), and practice putting it back together.

Ambitious Activities.

Pizza. If you have time and feel like running to the store, get a few simple ingredients and make a pizza together! I've even seen pizza making kits already to go at our local grocery store. A step easier than this would be to draw a big circle on a piece of paper and have your child draw what toppings they like on their pizza. This option is nice because it doesn't require leaving your home.

Practice Pouring into a Pot. Get two big pots and fill one with water. Using measuring cups, let your little one practice their pouring skills by moving water from one pot to the other.

- Be **Quiet**!
  - Be as quiet as you can and see what different noises you can hear. Try this inside and outside.
- Pretend to be a **Queen**
- **Quack** like a duck
- Draw a picture of a **Quilt**
  - You can use one paper, draw a quilt on it and try to make each square a different color. You can also use lots of different pieces of paper, color each paper a different color, and then put them together to form a bigger, paper quilt.
- Look up pictures of **Quills** (on a porcupine)
- **Quarter**
  - Show your child a quarter and explain that you use this to buy things. If you have several quarters, have your kiddo practice counting by counting how many you have.
- Look up pictures of **Quails**
- Ask **Questions**
  - "How old are you?" "What should we do today" "What food do you like" "What does that toy do?" Etc.
  - If possible, have your kiddo ask you questions as well.
- Be **Quick**!
  - Explain that quick means fast. Ask your child to do several things quickly (spin in a circle, nod their head, move their feet, blink quickly, etc.).
- **Q-tip** art
  - Use Q-tips as a paintbrush and paint a picture. You can also grab some glue and glue Q-tips onto a piece of paper in funny shapes and designs!

- **Read** a book together

- Locate items that are **Red**

- Count cars as they drive by on the **Road**
  - This is a great time to review road and sidewalk safety.

- Look up pictures of **Rollercoasters**
  - Pretend you are **Riding** on one.

- Hop like a **Rabbit**

- Have a **Race** or **Run** in place

- Play **Ring** around the **Rosies**

- Sing the children's song, "**Row, Row, Row** your Boat"

- Talk and move like a **Robot**

- Draw a picture of a **Rainbow**

- **Roll** around on the floor
  - Or **Roll** a ball back and forth.

- Look up pictures/videos of **Rockets**

- **Rice** dig
  - Empty a bag of uncooked rice into a big bowl. Hide a few small items in the rice and watch your child enjoy finding the items!

- **Roar** like a lion!

- Use a **Ruler** — practice measuring different toys together.

Ambitious Activity.

Rocks. There are SO many different activities that you can do with rocks! Below are different rock ideas. Some are extremely simple and some require a little more time and effort.

Rock Hunt – go on a walk and collect rocks.

Count Rocks – add some math into your letter learning and count the rocks you see.

Rock Wash – help your little one wash and polish up the special rocks they found.

Color/Paint Rocks – turn this into an art activity and let your child decorate the rocks however they want.

Pet Rock – turn your rock into a new "pet" by drawing a face and other details on it.

Ss

- Pretend to be **Snakes**
- **Smell** different things around your house
    - This is a good activity to do in the kitchen.
- **Sing Songs**
- Look up pictures of **Stars**
    - If possible, go look at real stars outside.
- Pretend to **Sleep** (and **Snore**)
- Help your kiddo locate their **Stomach**, **Shoulders**, **Shins** and **Spine**
- Locate items that are **Soft**
- **Stretch**
    - Stretch up high, down low, stretch your arms and legs, etc.
- Make **Silly** faces
- **Skip** together
- Practice **Sharing**
    - Have your child collect a few toys and practice sharing them and taking turns.
- Draw a picture of a **Spider**
- Look for **Spider** webs outside
- Practice **Scissor Skills**
    - Draw lines down a piece of paper and help your kiddo cut down the lines.

- Build a **Snowman**
  - If you are lucky enough to have snow at this time, build a snowman outside! If not, you can use playdough or cotton balls to build one or simply draw a picture of a snowman.

- Locate **Shoes** and **Socks**
  - Have your child practice putting these on by themselves.

- Draw a picture of the **Sun**

- **See** — Go on a walk and ask your munchkin to tell you what they see.

- **Spin** around in circles
  - Be careful you don't get too dizzy!

- Watch the **Sunset**

- Go outside and look for your **Shadow**.
  - Bring different toys/objects outside and look at the different shadows they make too.

- **Stand** up/**Sit** down
  - We make a game out of this where I say, "Stand up" and "Sit down" quickly and the girls try to keep up with what I'm saying!

Seasonal Activity: Spring

If it's Springtime when you are learning about the letter "S", talk about how nature changes in Spring (snow melting, flowers blooming, weather getting warm, etc). If possible, go outside and look at some of these changes as you talk about them.

Seasonal Activity: Summer

If it's Summer when you are learning about the letter "S", talk about fun activities you and your munchkin like to do during Summer and do one together! This could be drawing chalk pictures outside, going to the park, eating popsicles, etc.

Weather: Snow

If there happens to be snow on the ground when you are learning about the letter "S", there are lots of fun things you can do — sledding, build a snowman, just play in the snow! If you're not up to all the work of putting on snow clothes and going outside, you can simply open a door (that leads to the outside) and let your little one touch the snow.

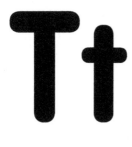

- Move like a **Turtle**

- Go outside and look for **Trucks**
    - You can go on a walk and search for one or just sit, wait, and hope one drives by.
    - Play with toy Trucks if you have them.

- Pretend to be a **Tiger**

- Locate your **Tummy**, **Toes**, **Teeth** and **Tongue**

- **Ticklefight**!

- Make a **Tent** (using blankets, sheets, etc.)

- Make **Train** noises

- Practice counting to **Ten**
    - Use fingers and toes to help count!

- Brush your **Teeth**

- Play with **Toys**
    - Or clean up the toys.

- **Talk** to each other
    - Take time to just sit and have a conversation with your little one.

- Look up pictures of **Tractors**

- Name animals that have **Tails**
    - You can look up pictures of these animals as you name them off or pretend to be these animals!

- **Tap** your fingers
  - Try this on different surfaces and listen for the differences.

- Locate **Trees** as you go on a walk together

Holiday: Thanksgiving

I LOVE Thanksgiving — Eating food all day, spending time with family and the excitement of Christmas around the corner! If you are learning about the letter "T" close to Thanksgiving, take advantage of it! You can talk to your child about Thanksgiving and name off yummy foods you want to make. You can pretend to be turkeys and gobble around the house together. We like to trace our hands onto a piece of paper and color it to look like a turkey (the tracing of your thumb is the turkeys head/face and the rest of your traced fingers are the feathers). You can also tell your little one things that you are thankful for and ask them what things they are thankful for.

Like the other vowels, "U" makes more than one sound. It makes a long sound where "U" says its name, as in the word "unicorn". It also makes a short sound where "U" sounds like "uh", as in the word "under".

- Crawl **Under** something
  - Under the table, under a chair, under the bed, etc.
  - If you don't have many options big enough to go under, have your child pick a small toy and put that under different places.

- Hide **Under** blankets

- Look up pictures of **Unicorns**

- Throw something **Up** in the air
  - Use something soft and easy to catch.

- Open an **Umbrella**
  - If you don't have one, look up pictures of umbrellas and pretend to be holding one in the rain.

- **Underwear**
  - Your child will probably giggle at this silly one! Ask them if they can find a pair of underwear from their room all by themselves. If your child isn't wearing underwear yet, use this as an opportunity to talk about transitioning from diapers to underwear.

- Draw an **Underwater** scene (sand, fish, turtles, coral, etc.)

- Look up pictures/videos of **Volcanoes**
- Locate **Vegetables** in the kitchen
  - You can also take a trip to the grocery store for this one.
- Have your munchkin help you **Vacuum**
- Listen to the sounds a **Violin** makes and pretend to play one.
  - We don't have a violin, so we look up what a violin sounds like on my phone.
- Pretend to be a **Vet**
  - Explain that a vet is a doctor for animals. Talk about how animals might get hurt and how we can help them feel better. Pretend to be a vet for a "sick" stuffed animal or toy.
- Show your child what **Veins** are
  - It's easy to locate the veins on your wrist.
- **Vest**
  - If you or your kiddo has a vest find it and throw it on!
- Locate **Vents** in your house
  - Explain that vents are where air comes out of. Go on an adventure to find vents around your house!
- **Voice** — practice using your quiet voice and your loud voice.
- **Vase**
  - Show your child what a vase is and let them fill the vase up with something.

Holiday: Valentine's Day

I'm not a huge fan of this holiday, but it's fun to celebrate with kids I think! We like to make homemade Valentine cards. We give these to family members or drop them off to someone we think might be surprised to get one! I love showing my girls ways we can make someone's day that doesn't cost any money.

- **Wiggle** like a **Worm**

- **Watch** a movie together

- **Wrap** up in a blanket and get **Warm**

- **Wash** your hands

- **Whisper**
  - Only talk to each other using whisper voices or whisper sing the ABC's.

- Look up pictures of **Walruses** and **Whales**

- Drink **Water**

- Locate items that are **White**

- **Wash** the dishes or clothes together
  - This gives you a chance to get the dishes or laundry going while still being with your munchkin, talking to them, and helping them learn.

- Go on a **Walk** and feel the **Wind**
  - Point out leaves and grass blowing in the wind.

- Locate (or count) the **Windows** in your house

- Pretend you have a magic **Wand**

- Draw a picture of a spider **Web**
  - Try to find a spider web outside.

- **Whistle**
  - I'm 28 and still have no idea how to whistle! If you can't whistle, just make the best fake whistle noise you can.

- Pretend you have **Wings** and can fly
  - Talk about different animals/insects that have wings.

- Get **Wet**
  - This can be as simple as filling up the bathtub a little bit and getting your feet wet.

- **Writing** — practice writing your little one's name together

- **Workout** together

- **Weather**
  - Talk about the current weather. Ask your kiddo what their favorite weather is. Draw pictures of different types of weather.

Ambitious Activity.

Make special Waffles! These aren't your typical butter and syrup waffles. I'm talking about chocolate chips, fruit, sprinkles, and lots of whipped cream!

Seasonal Activity: Winter

If it happens to be Winter when you are learning about the letter "W", talk to your little one about things that happen in Winter. Examples of this are it gets dark earlier, the weather turns cold, it might snow, etc.

- **X** marks the spot
  - On several pieces of paper draw an "X". Hide these in one room of your house. Tell your child they are going on a treasure hunt to find all the "X's".

- Look up pictures of **X-rays**
  - Explain that X-rays can show us what is inside our bodies.

- Look up pictures of Fo**X**es

- Locate Bo**X**es around your house
  - Let your child open them up and see what's inside!

- Show your munchkin a picture of a **Xylophone** and pretend to play one together.

- Locate items that are **Yellow**

- Pretend to **Yawn**

- Find (or just talk about) food that you and your child think is **Yummy** and **Yucky**

- Look up pictures of **Yaks**

- Draw a picture of **Yourself**

- **Yell**!
  - Not in a mean way — just for fun!

- Ask **Yes**/No questions (that you think your child will probably respond "yes" to).

- **Yoga** poses
  - There are simple yoga videos online or you can make up your own poses!

Zz

- Locate items that have **Zippers** and practice zipping
  - Clothes, bags, wallets, etc.
- Look up pictures of **Zebras**
- Pretend to be **Zombies**
- Make a **Zero** with your hand.
  - Explain that you have zero when you have no more. Put a few items on the floor and then take them away. As you take them away explain to your child that now you have "zero". Practice this several times using different items. Have your kiddo practice showing you this as well.
- Talk about animals at the **Zoo**
  - And pretend to be them!
- Bu**ZZ** like a bee
- Draw pictures of **Zig-zags**
- **Zoom** toy cars around on the floor

The following pages (63 – 119) include the
ABC Coloring and Writing page for each letter.
Tear these pages out for easier use.
Enjoy!

Astronaut

A a

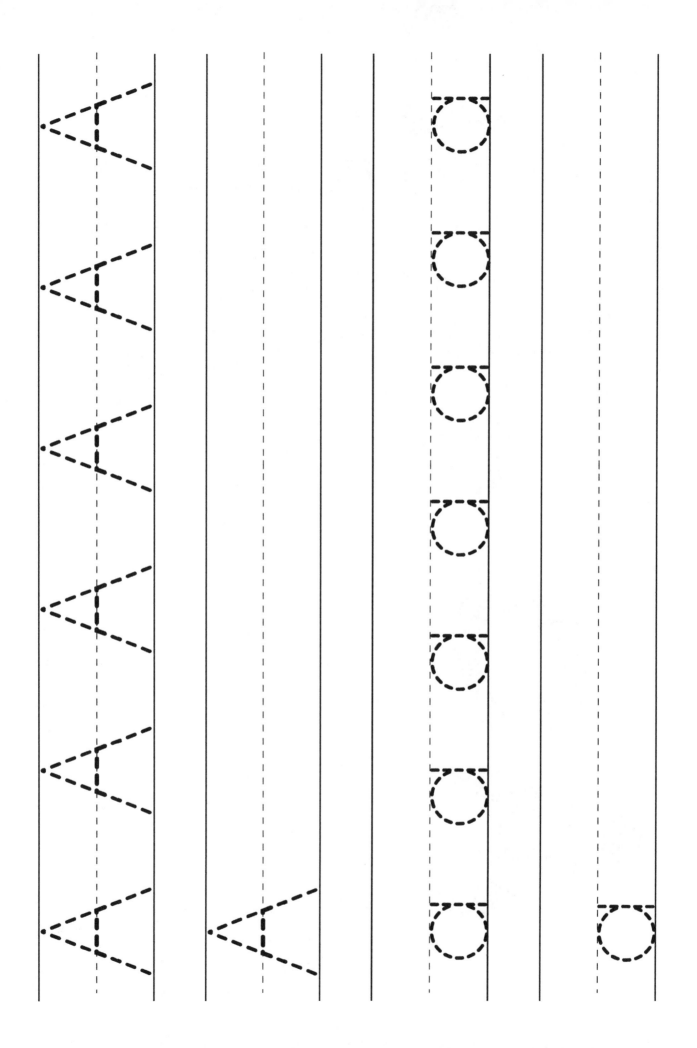

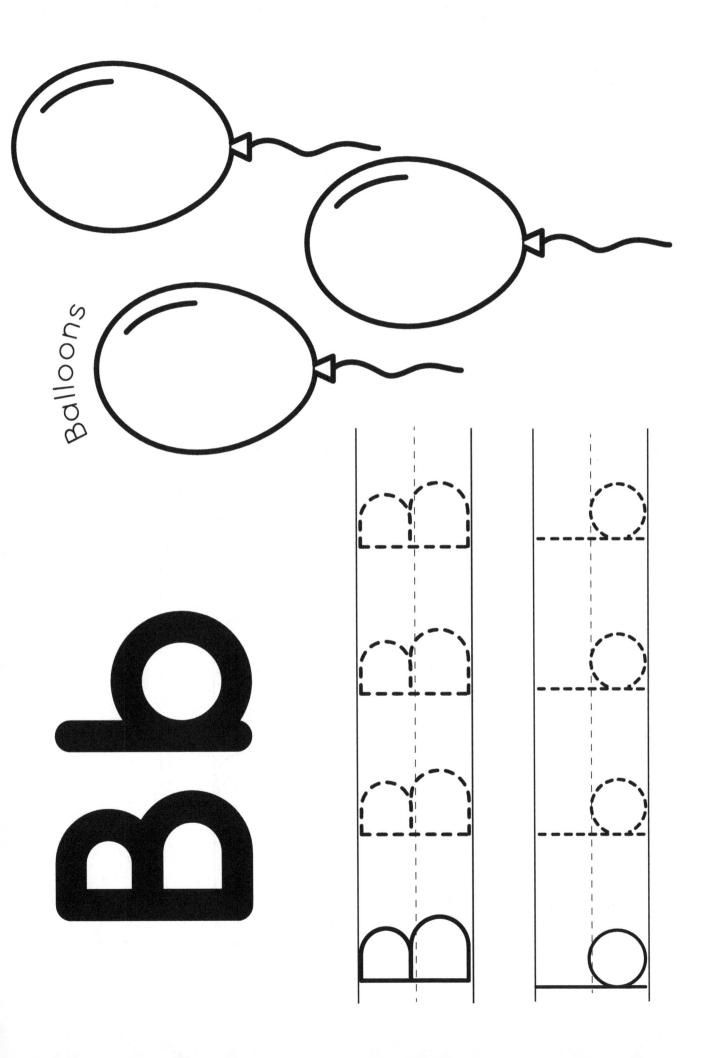

Balloons

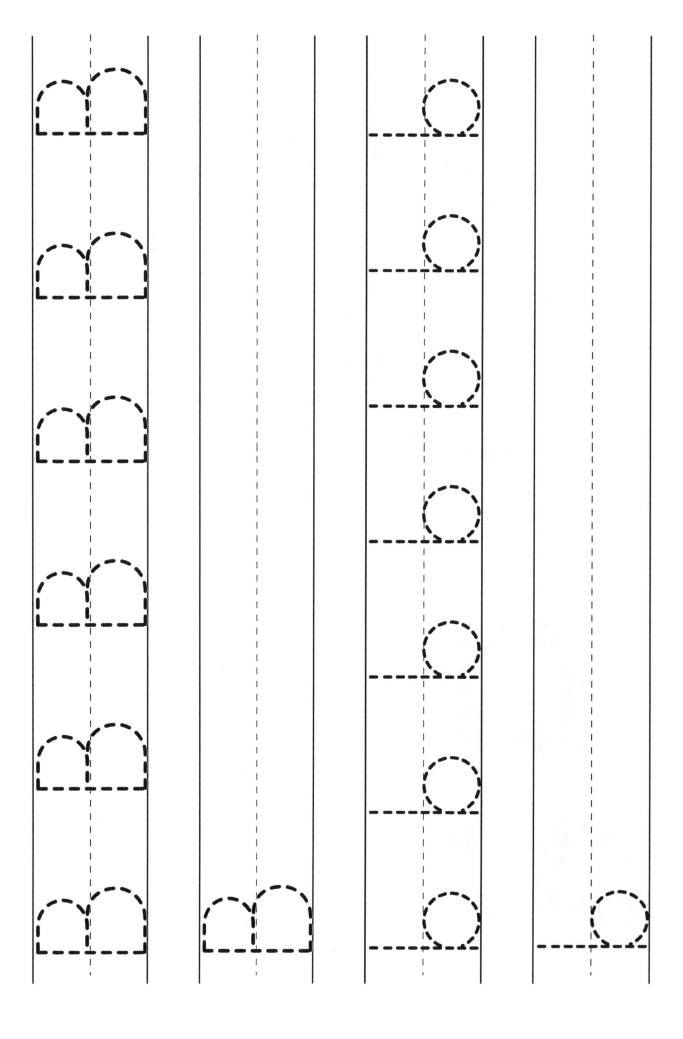

Castle

C c

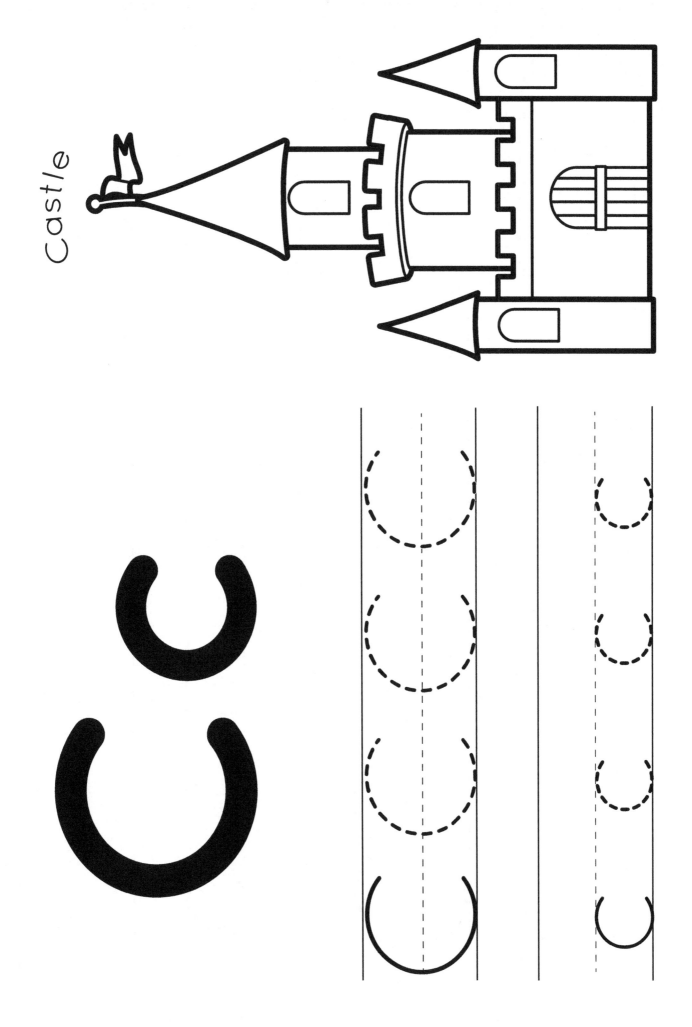

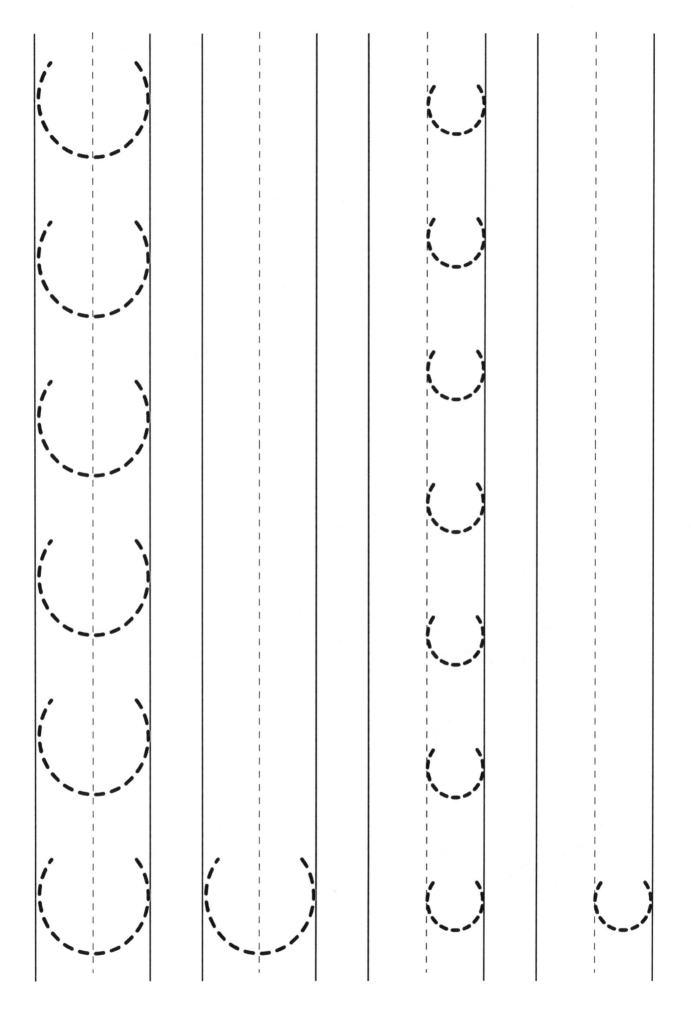

Dinosaur

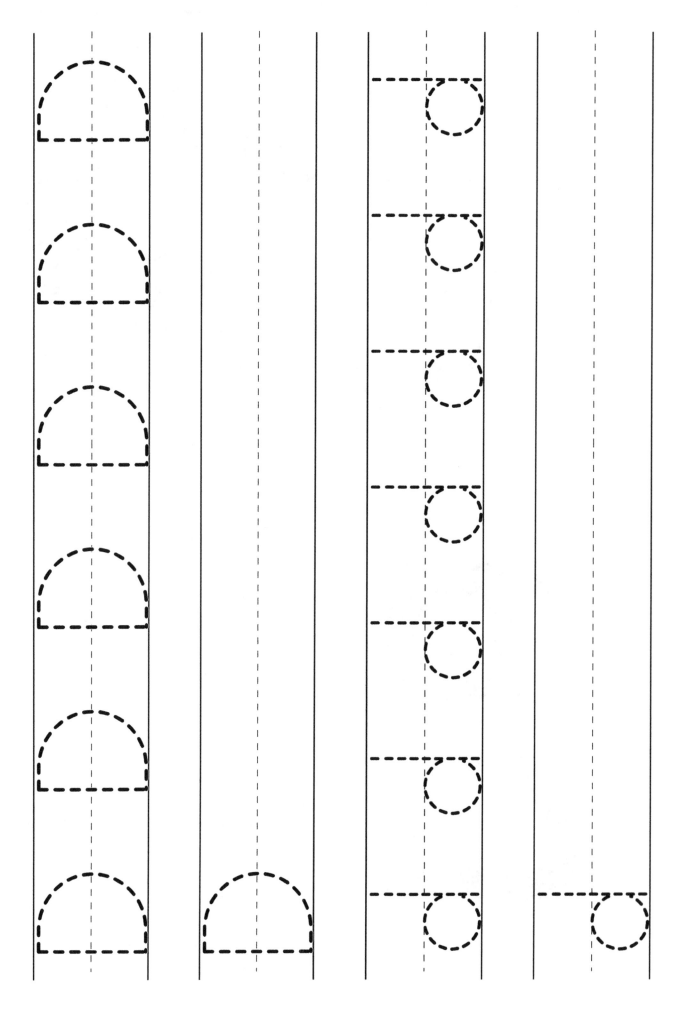

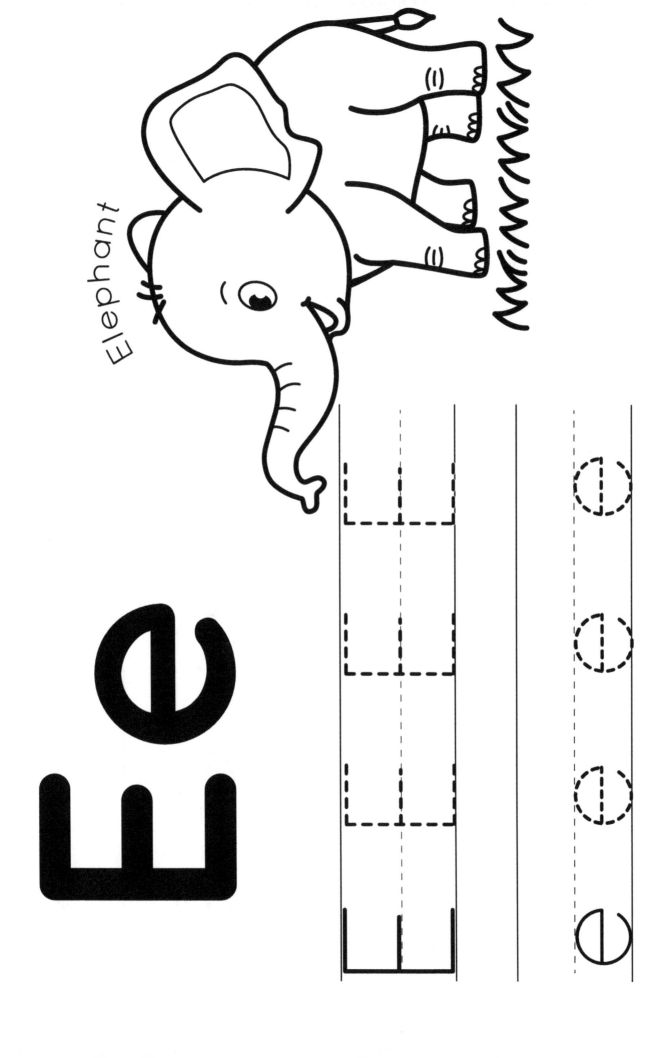

Elephant

E e

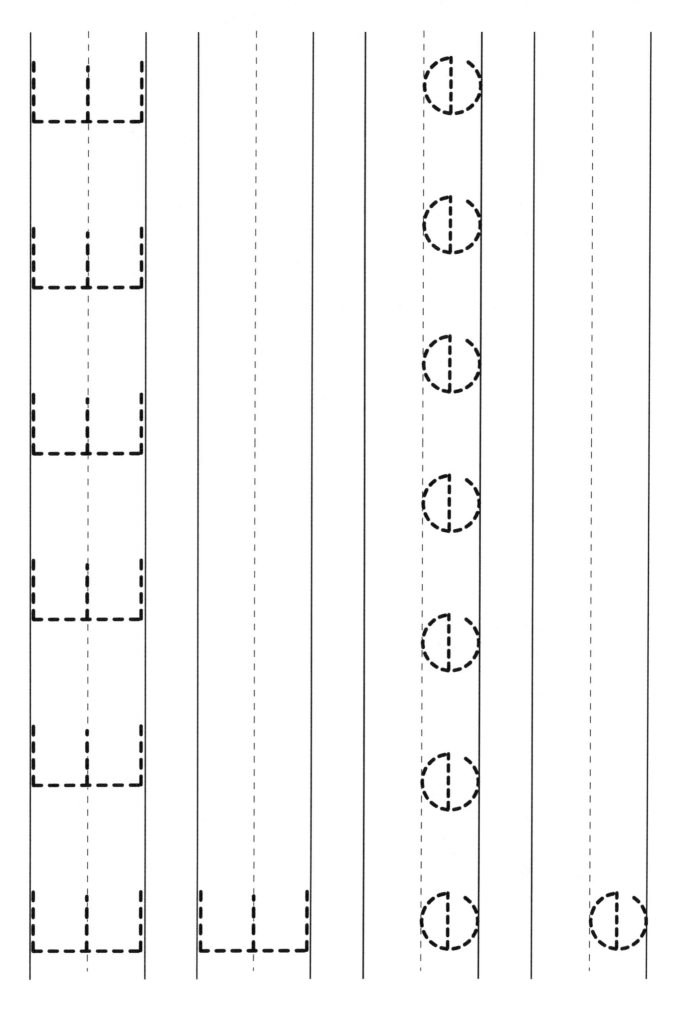

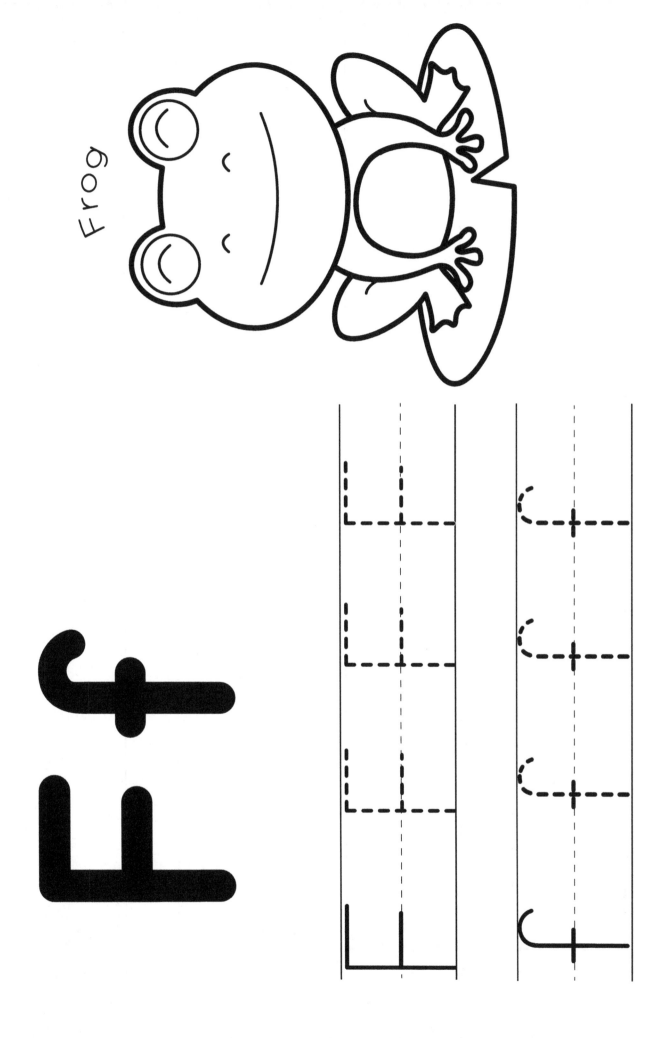

Frog

F f

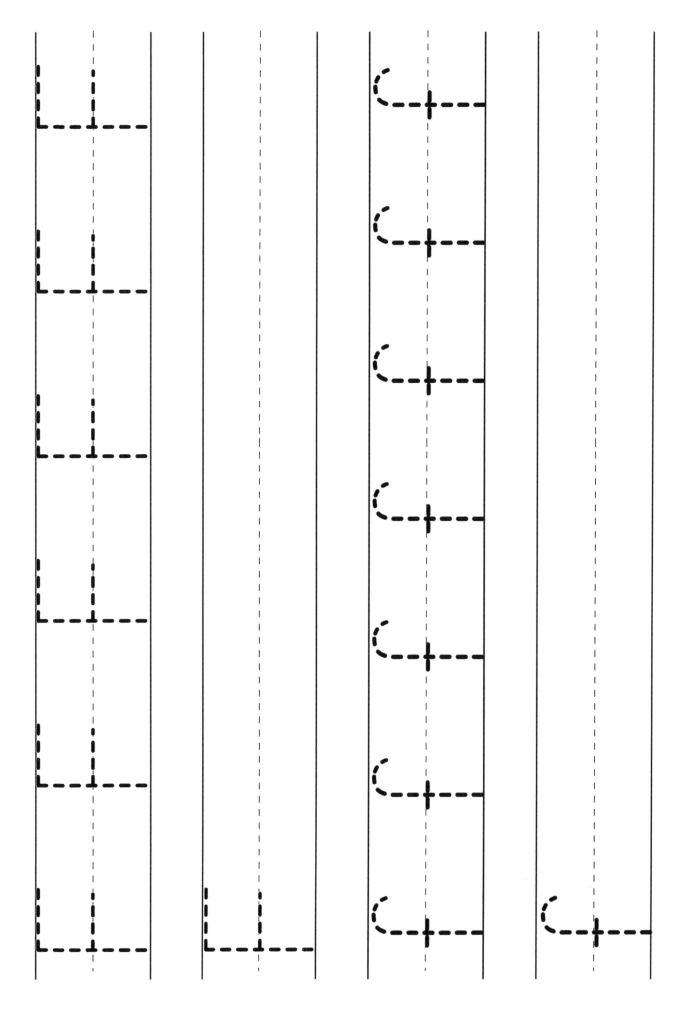

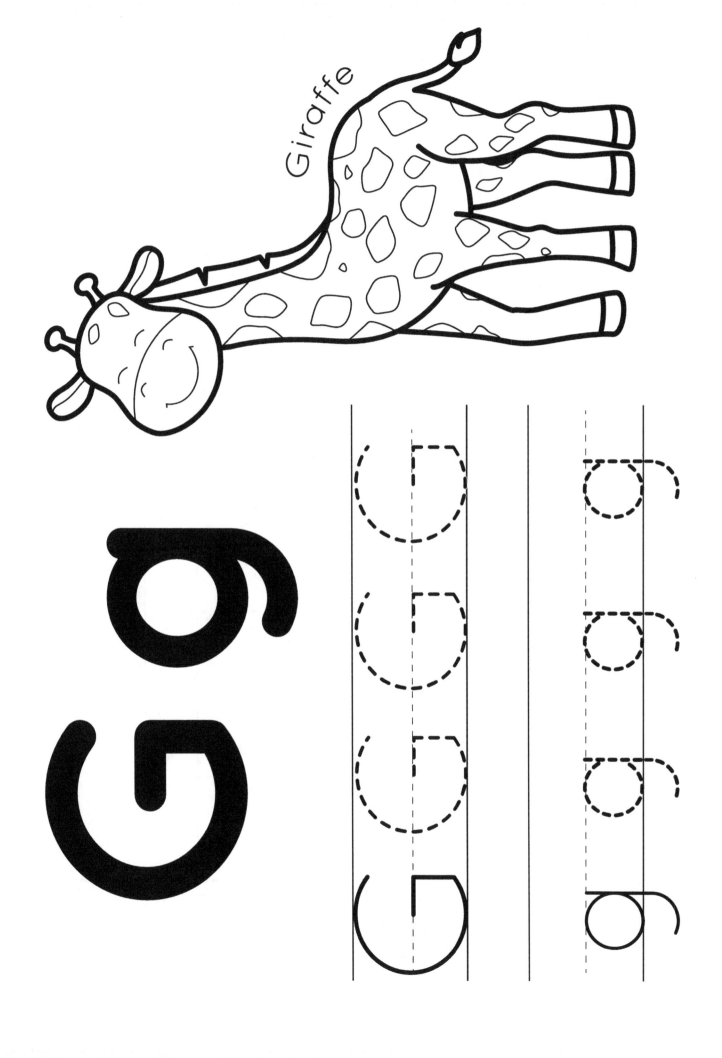

Giraffe

G g

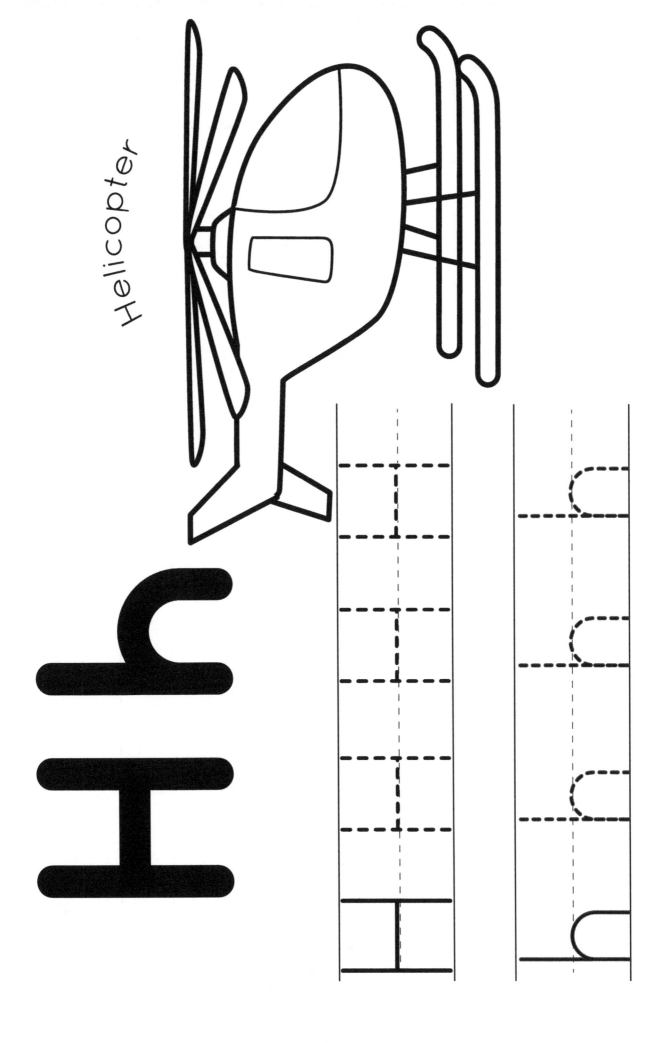

Helicopter

H h

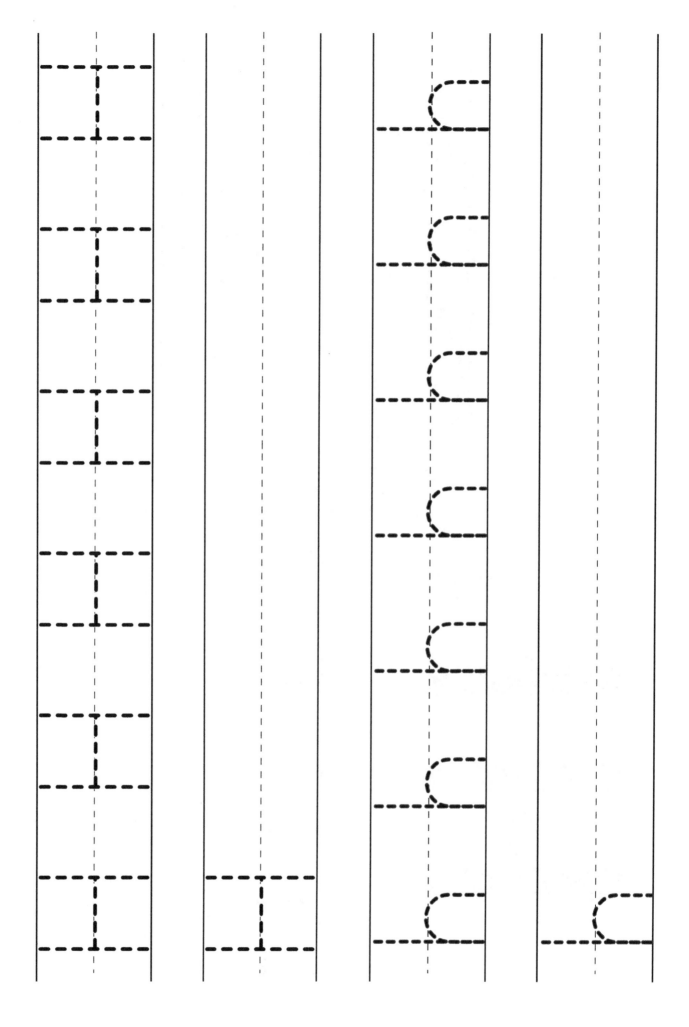

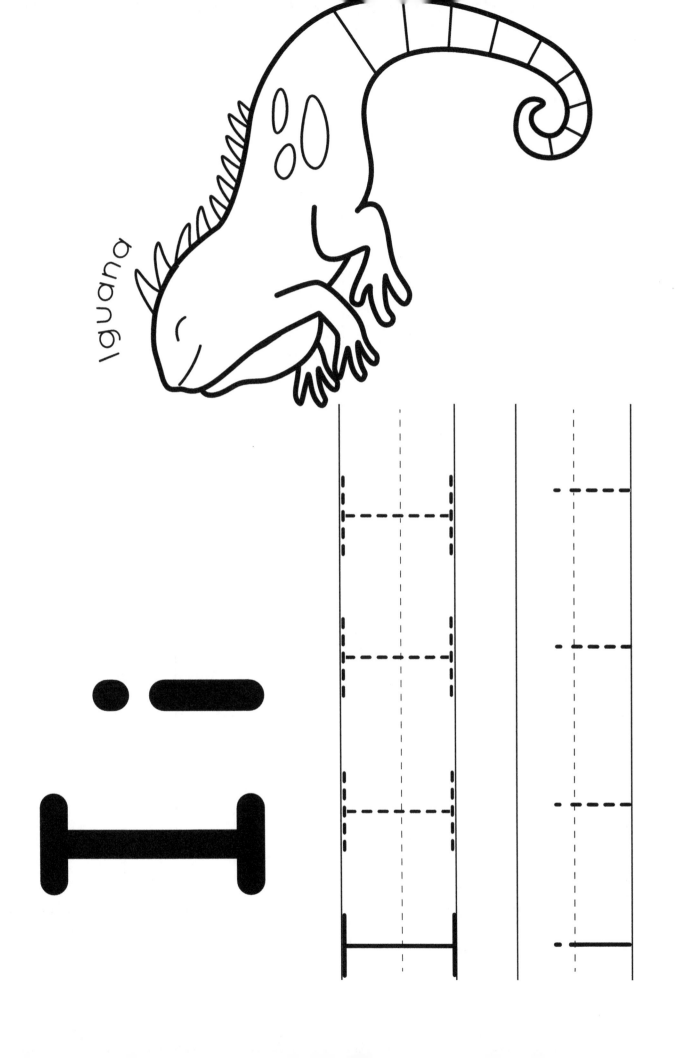

Iguana

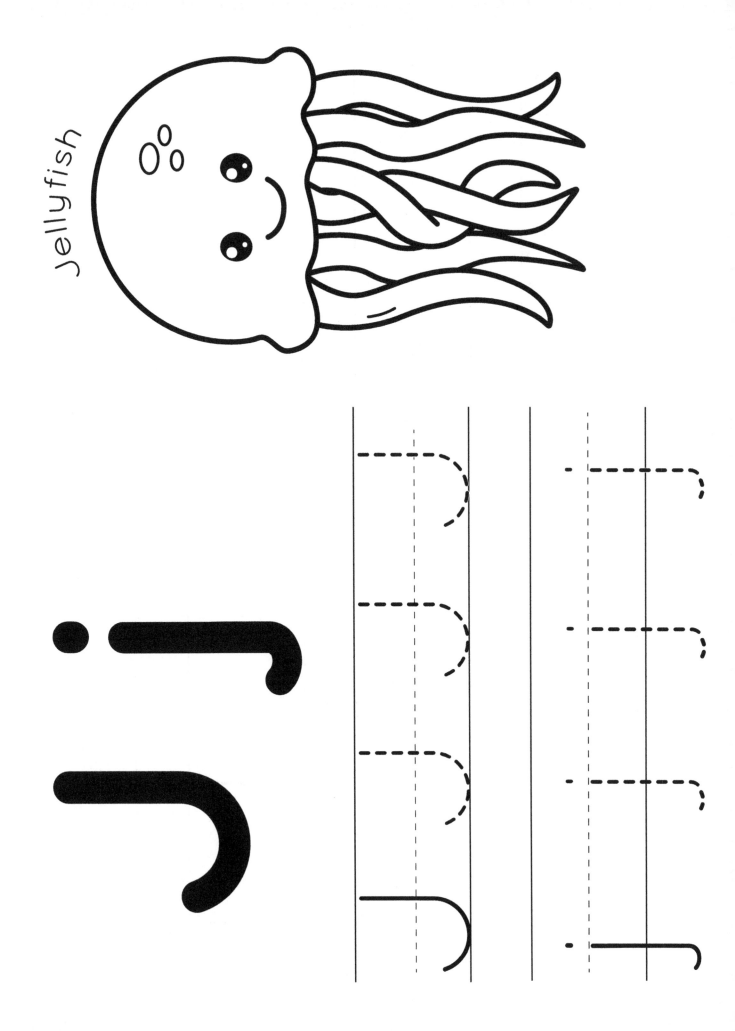

jellyfish

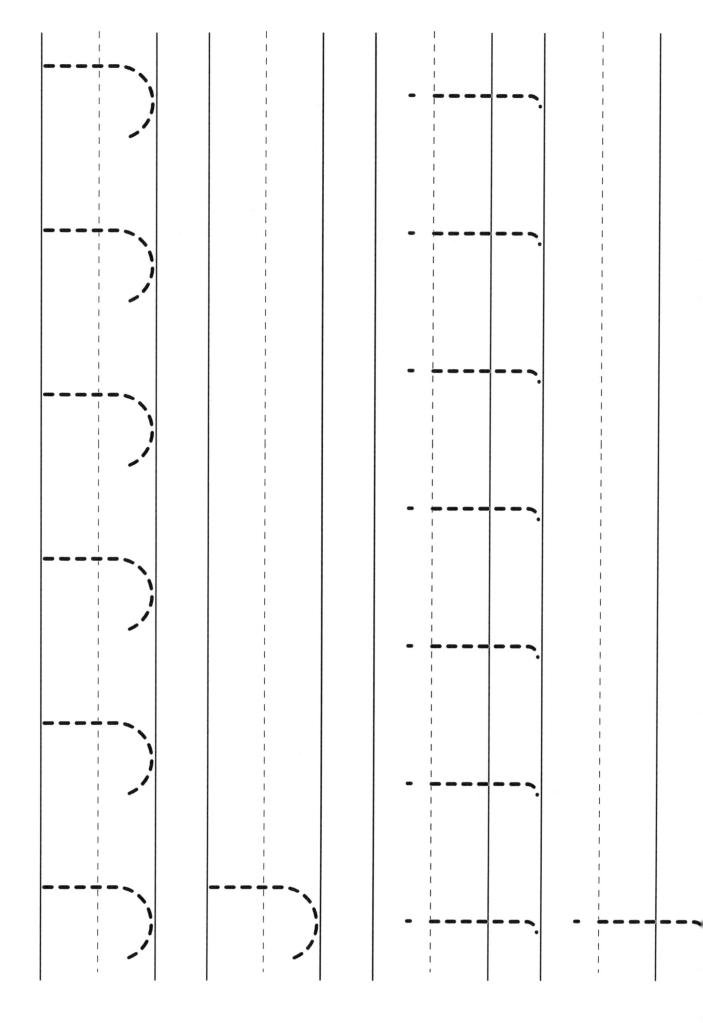

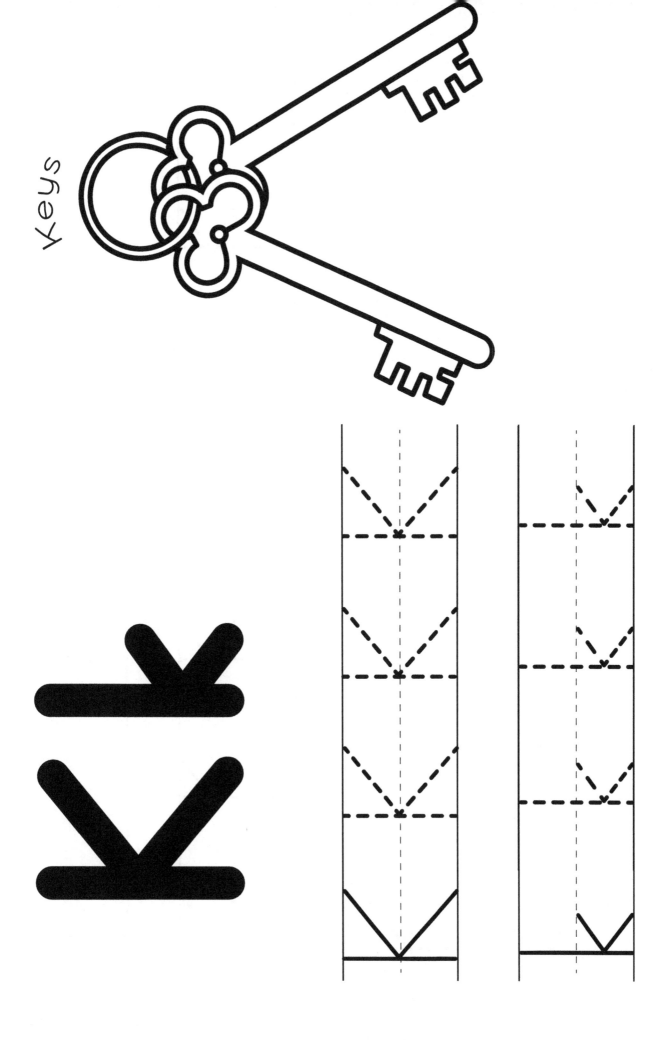

keys

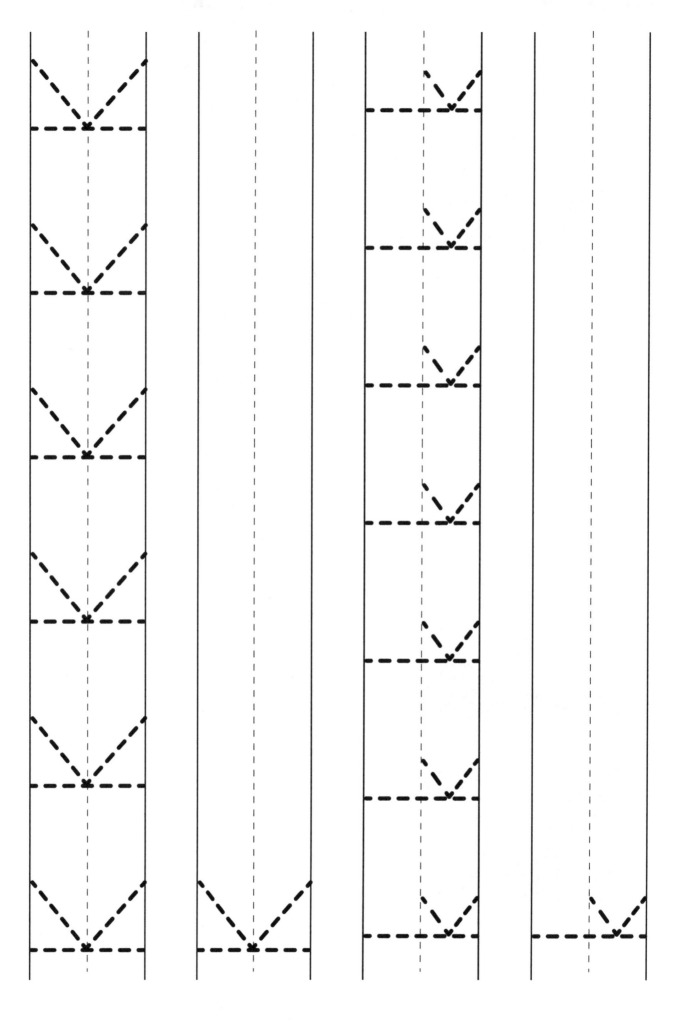

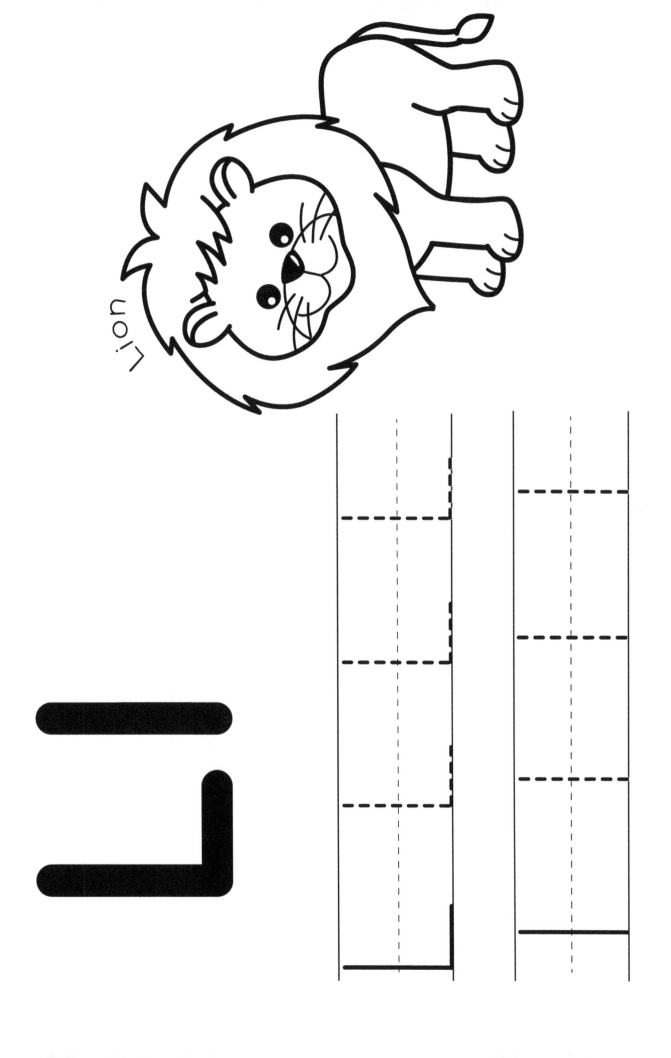

Lion

Monkey

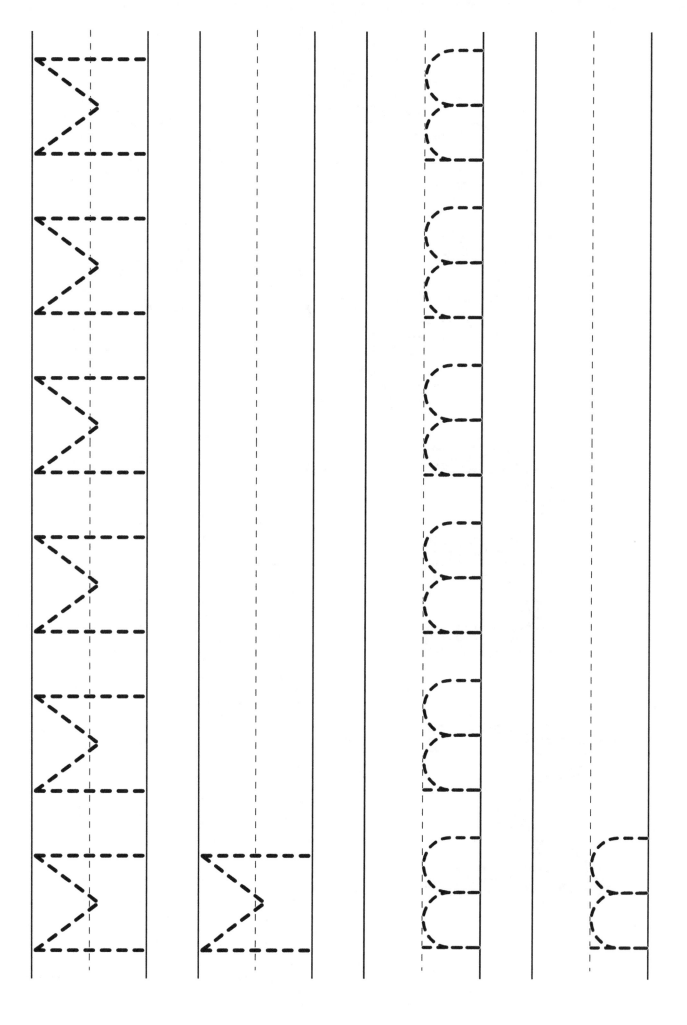

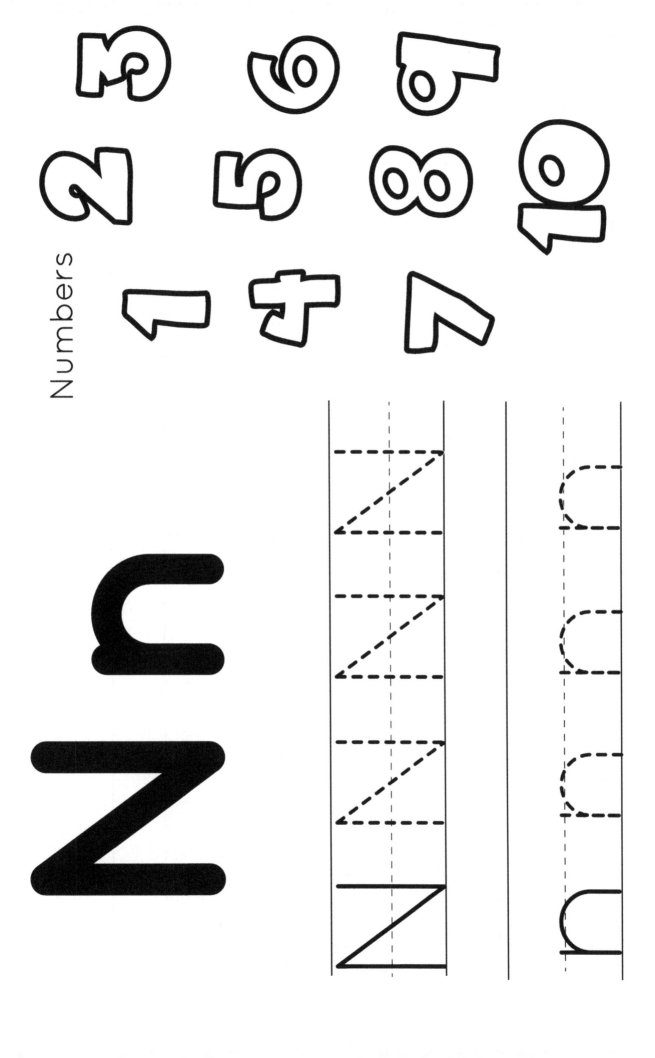

Numbers

N n

N N N N N N U U U U U

octopus

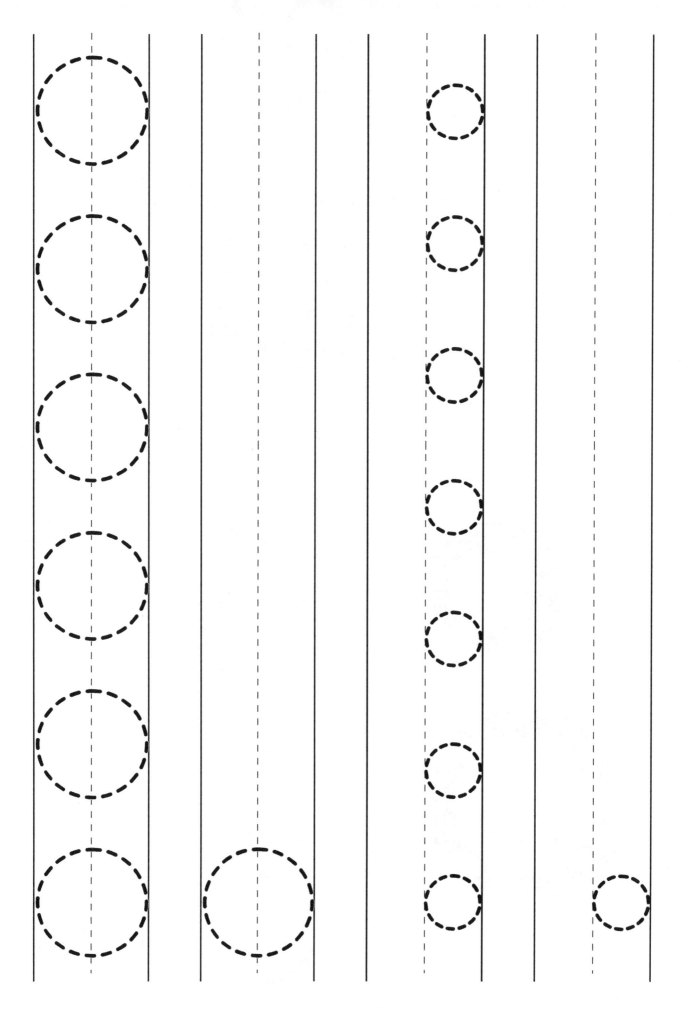

Pirate

P p

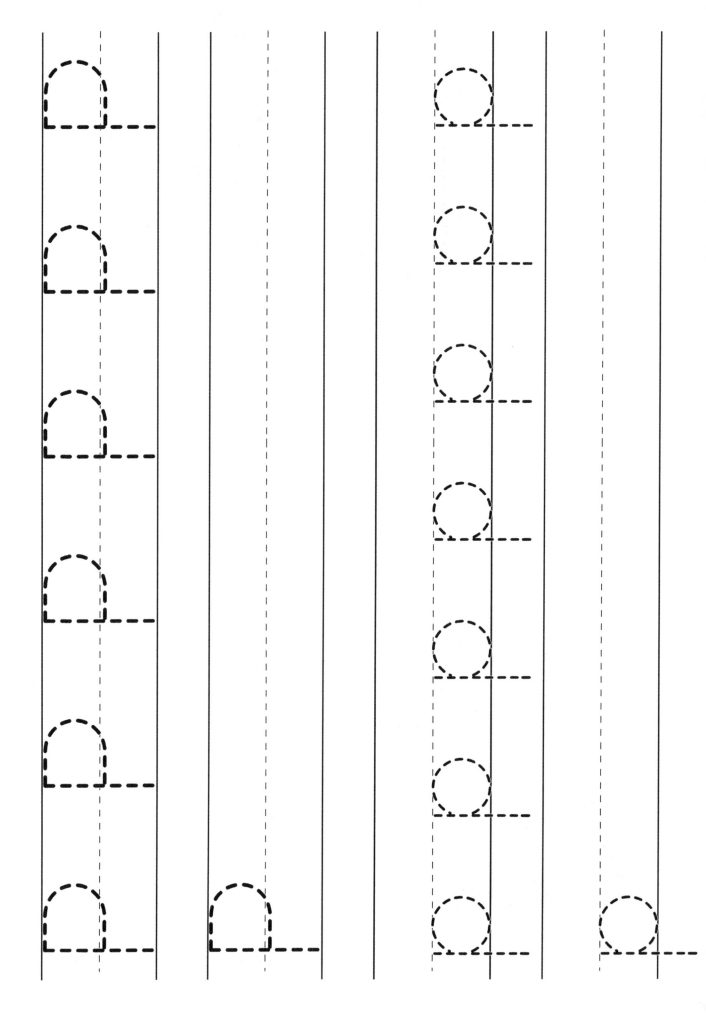

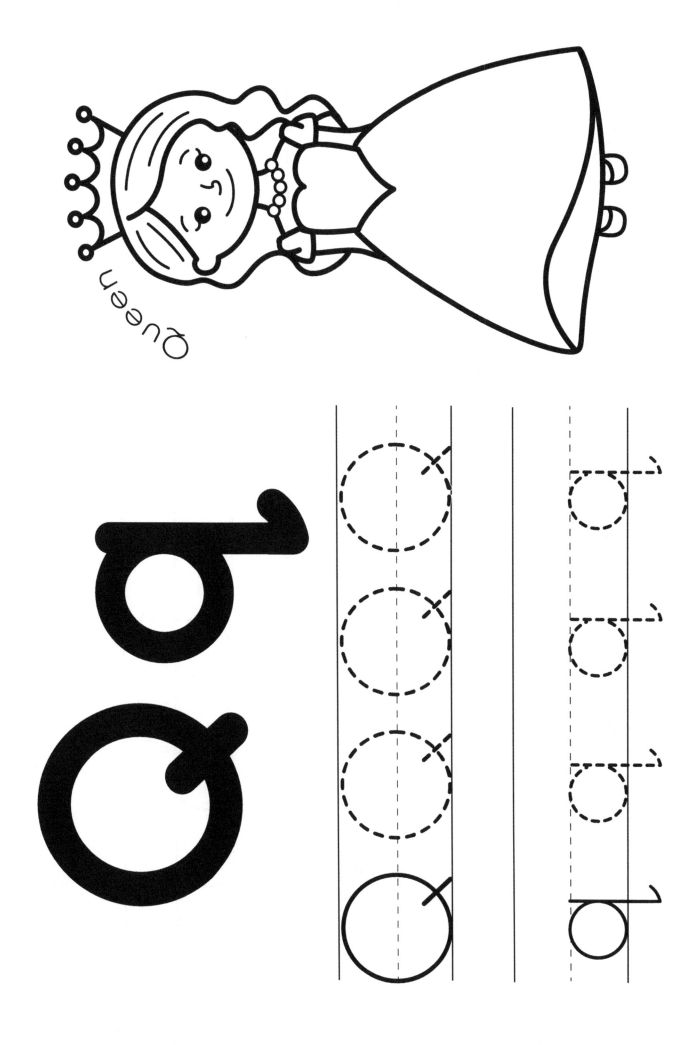

Queen

Q q

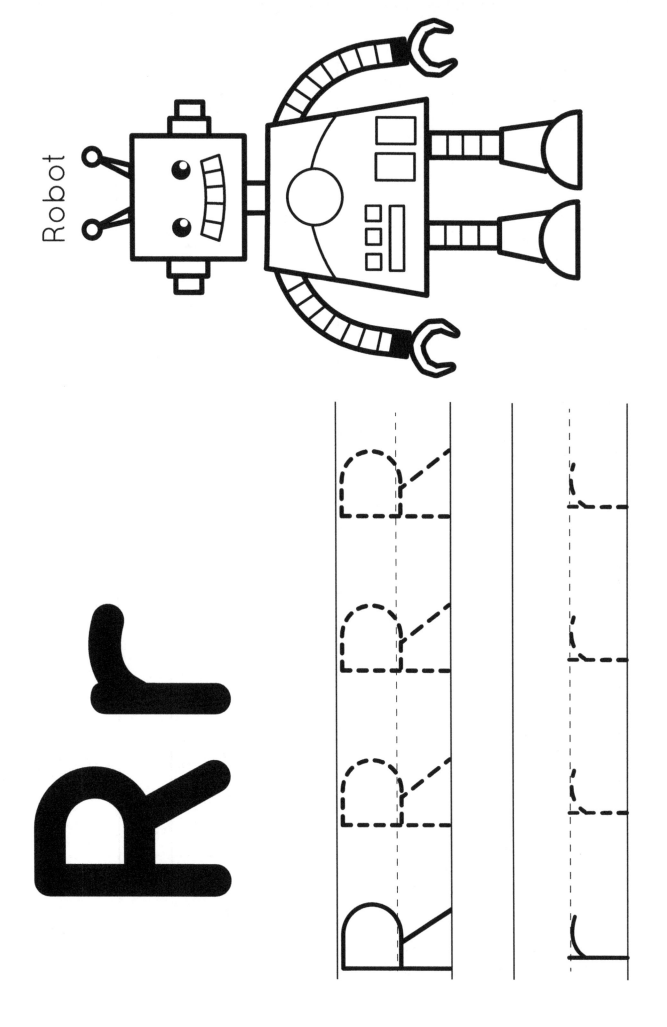

Robot

R r

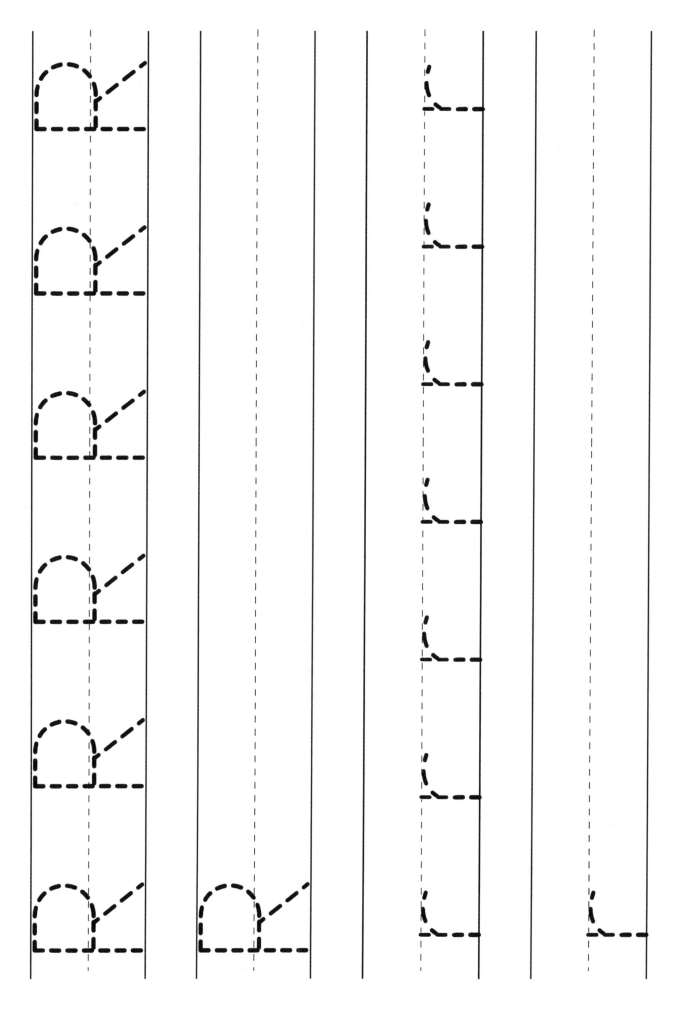

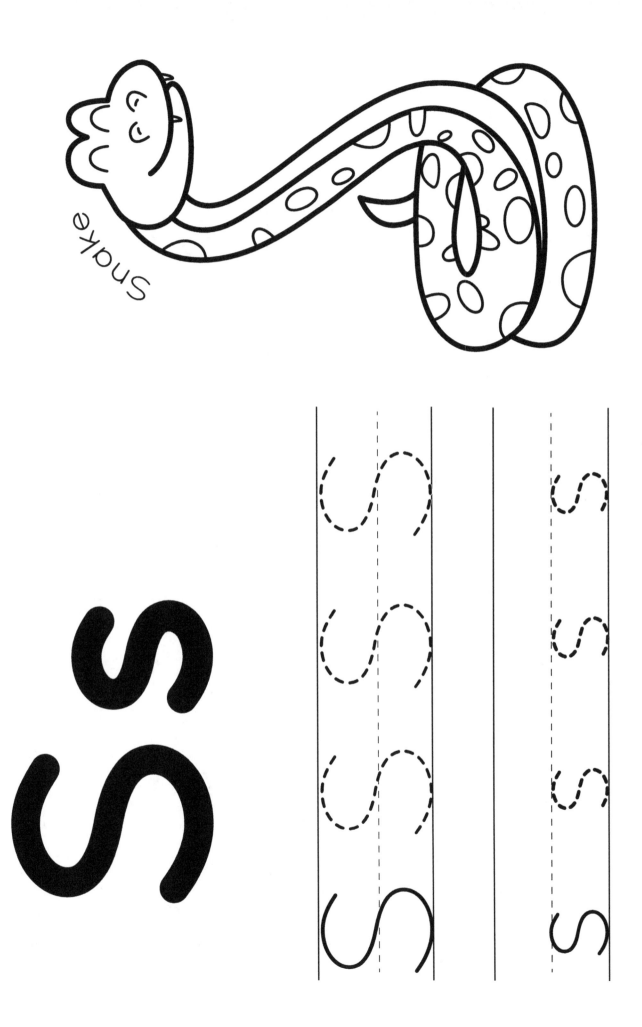

Snake

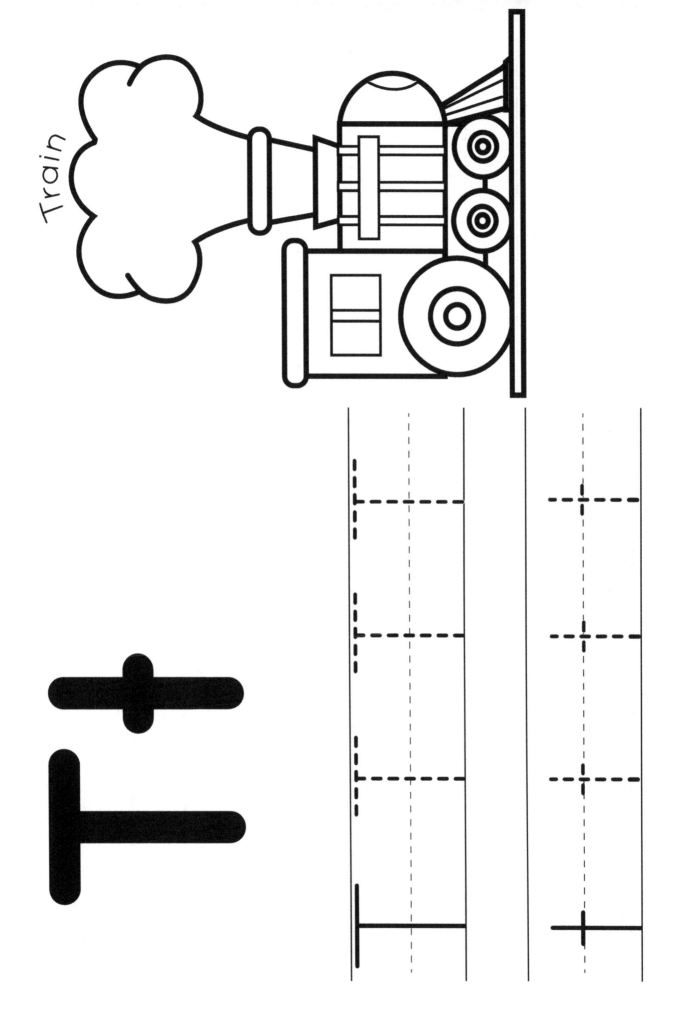

Train

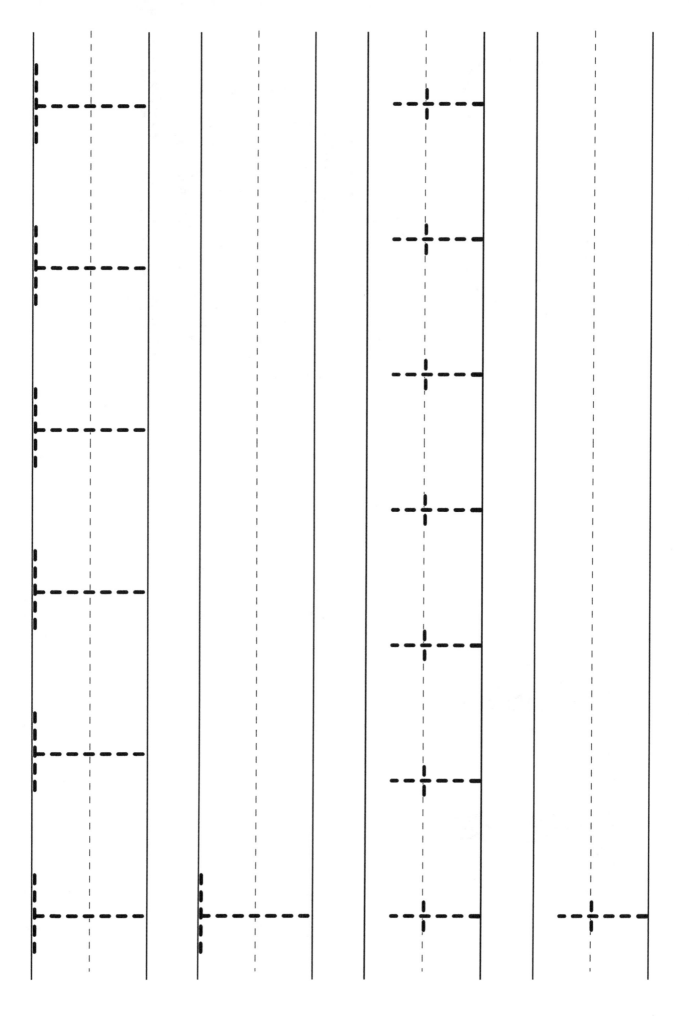

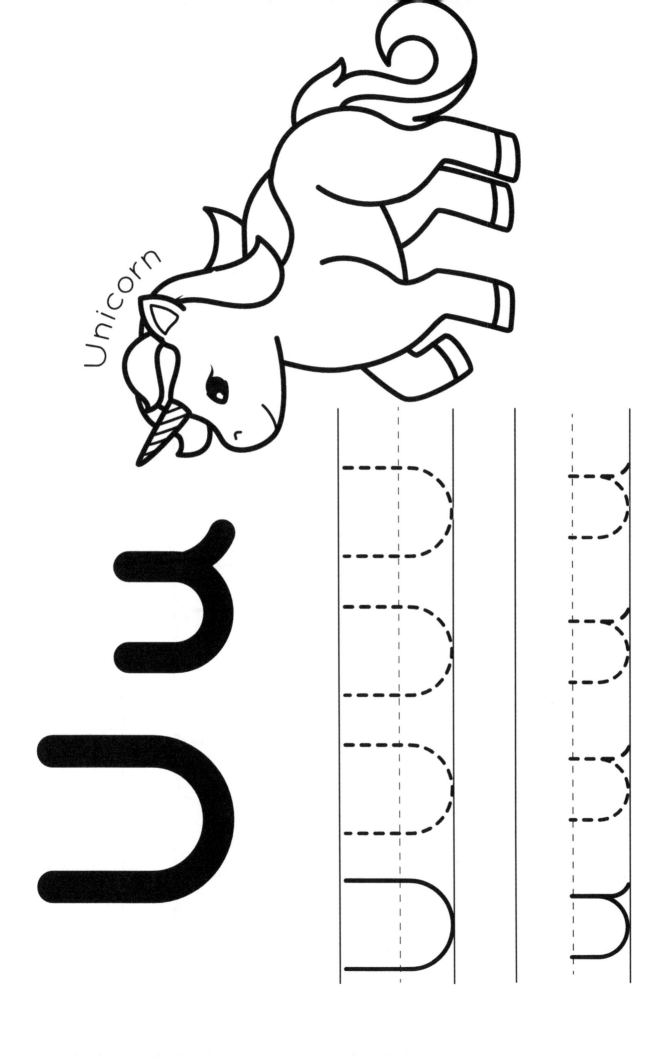

Unicorn

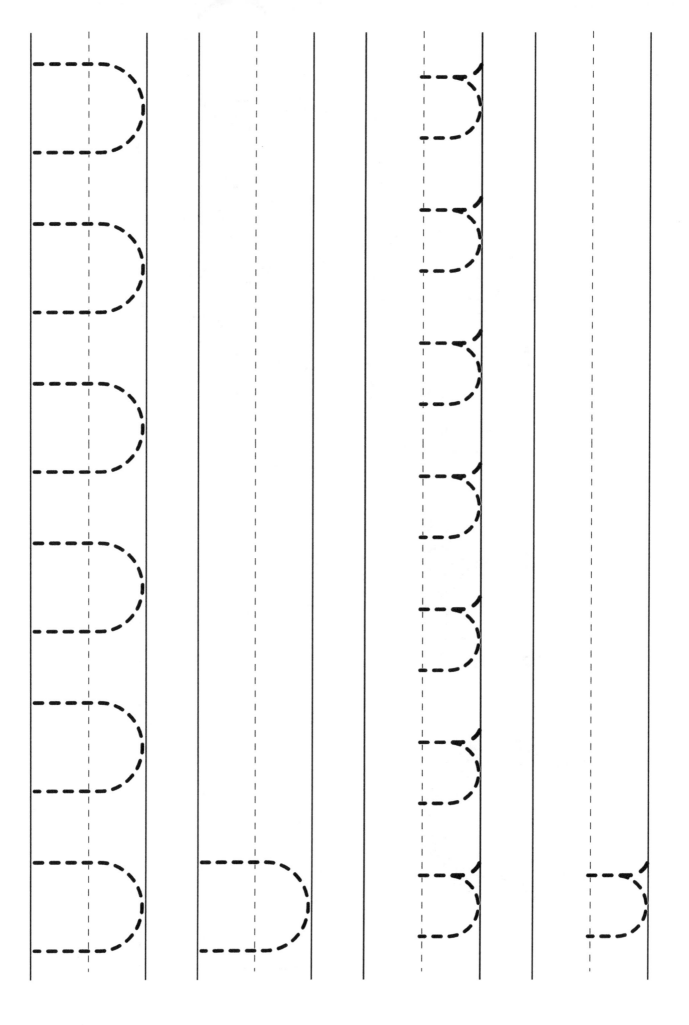

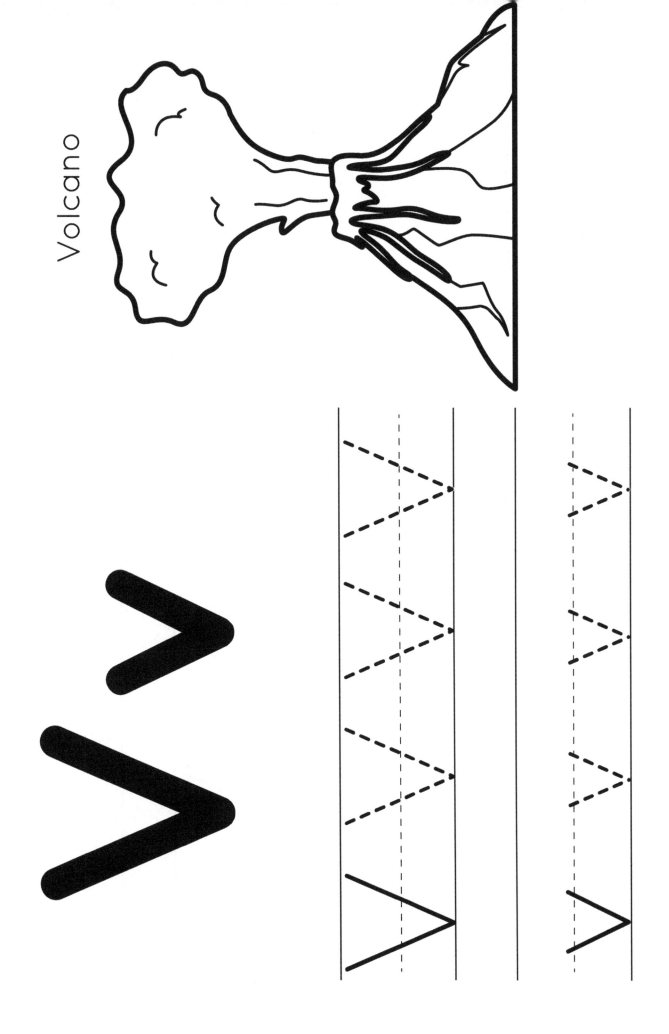

Volcano

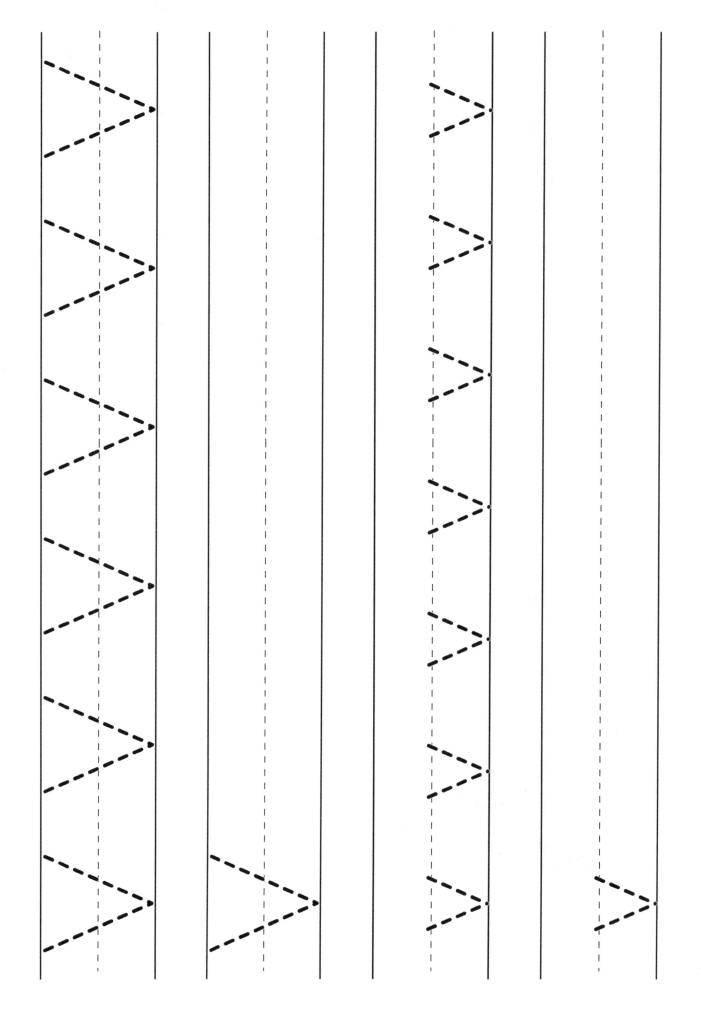

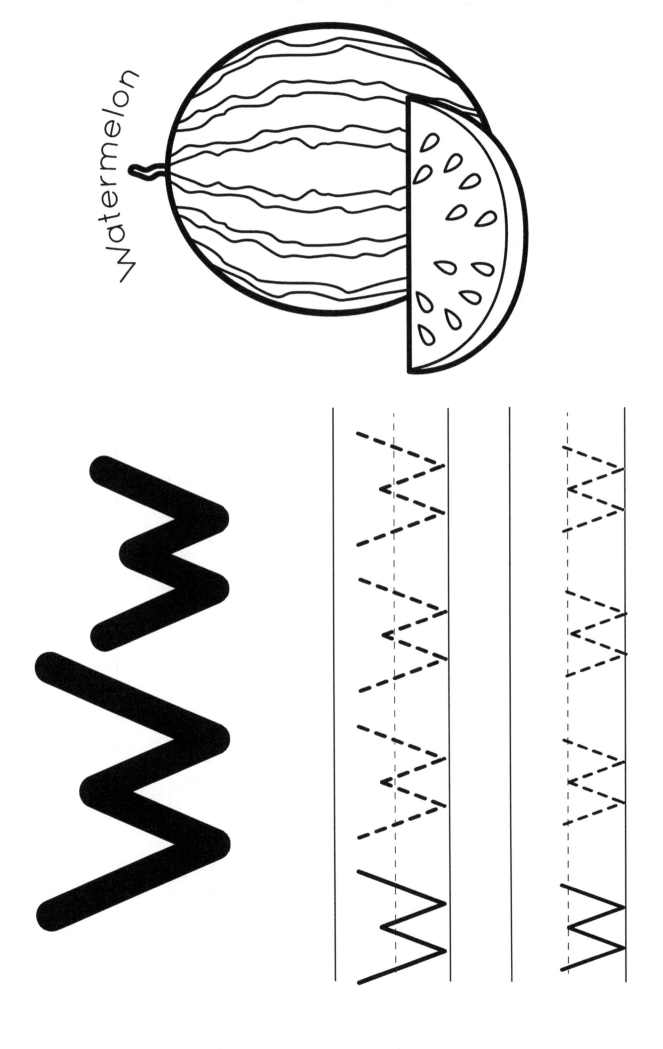

Watermelon

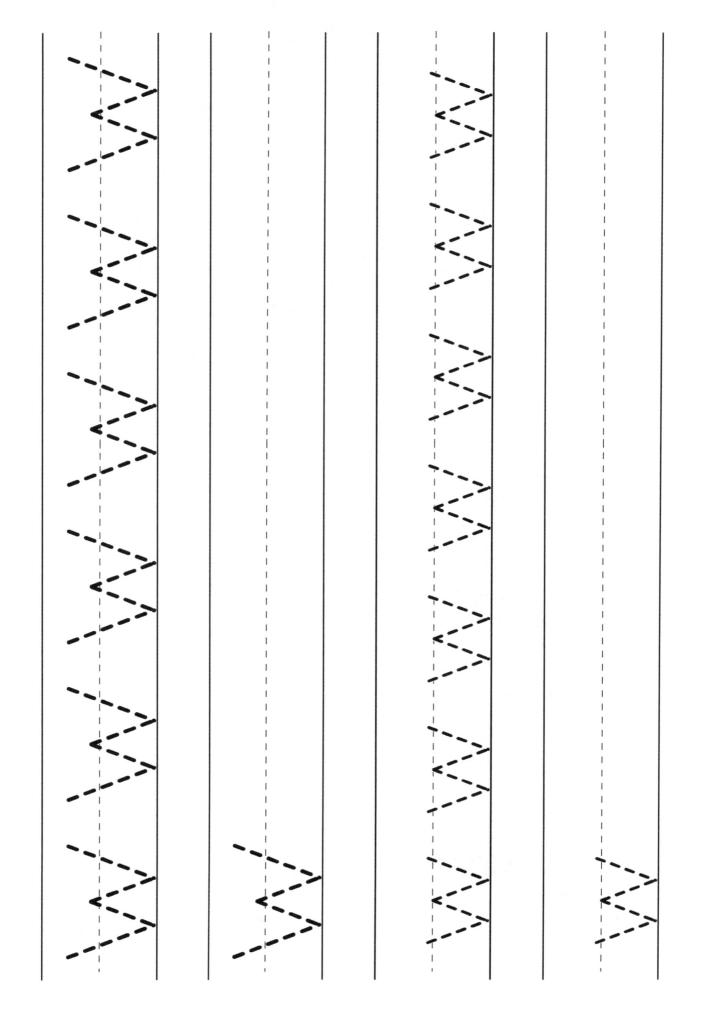

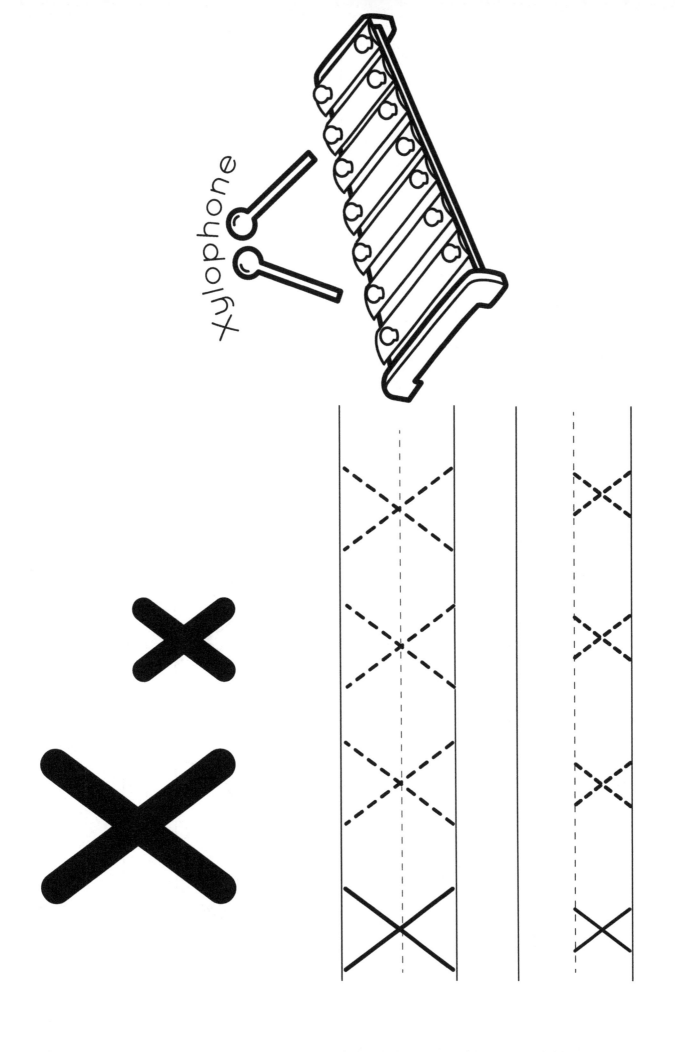

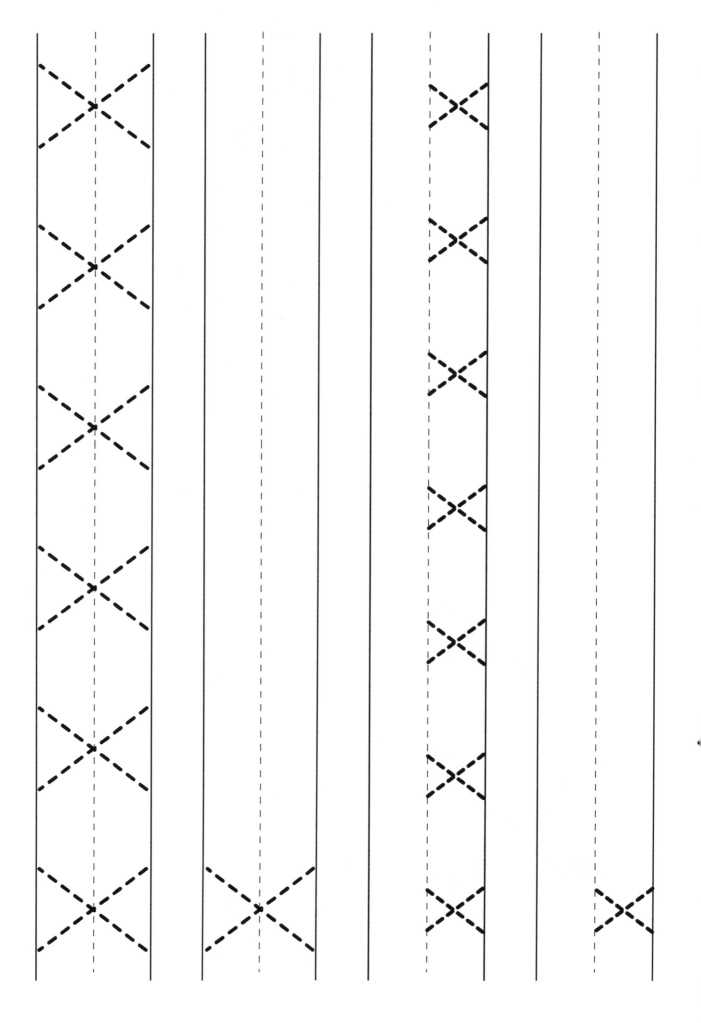

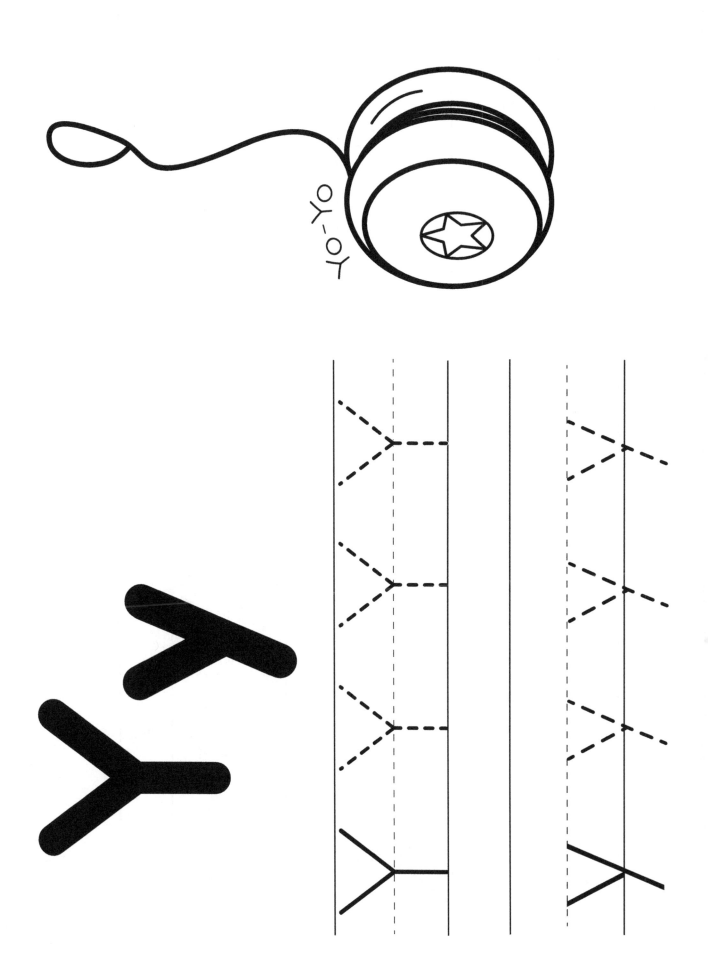

YO-YO

Zz

zombie

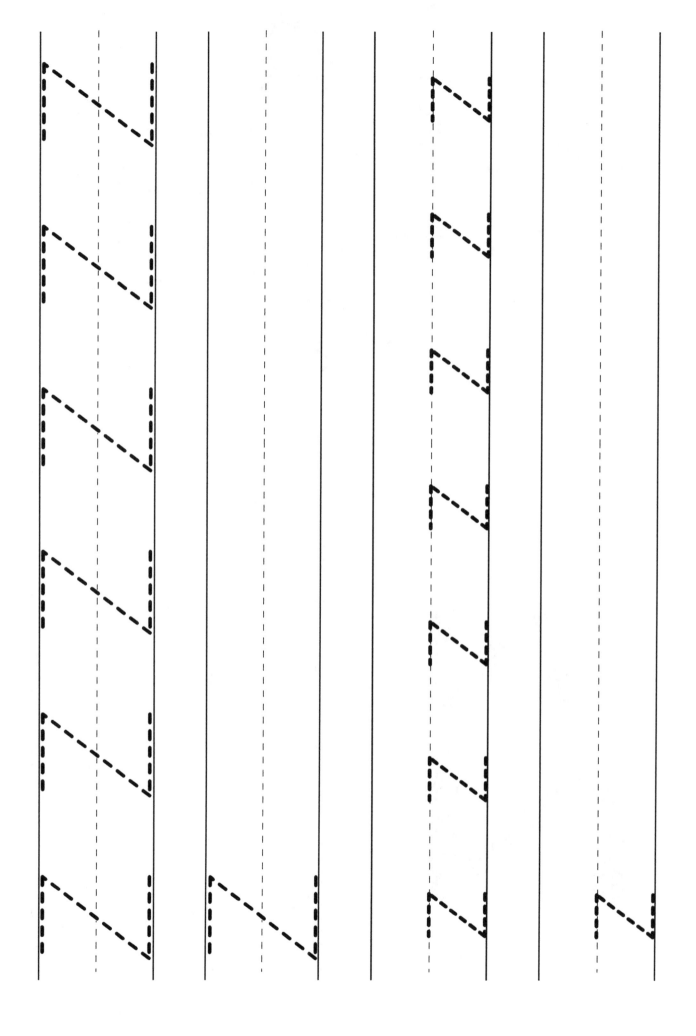

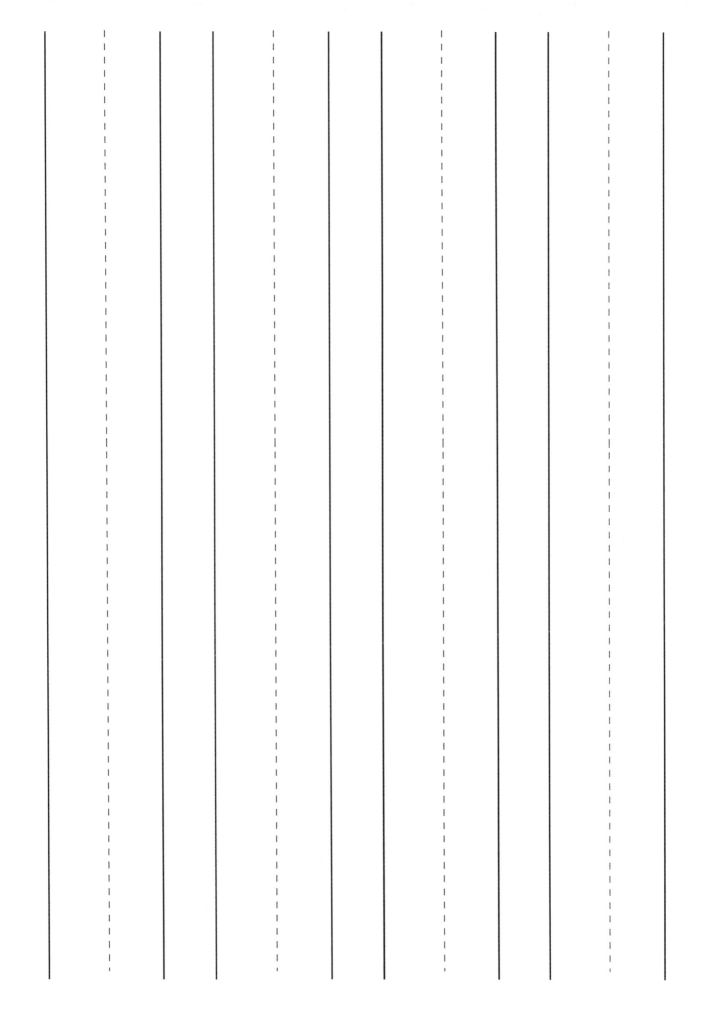

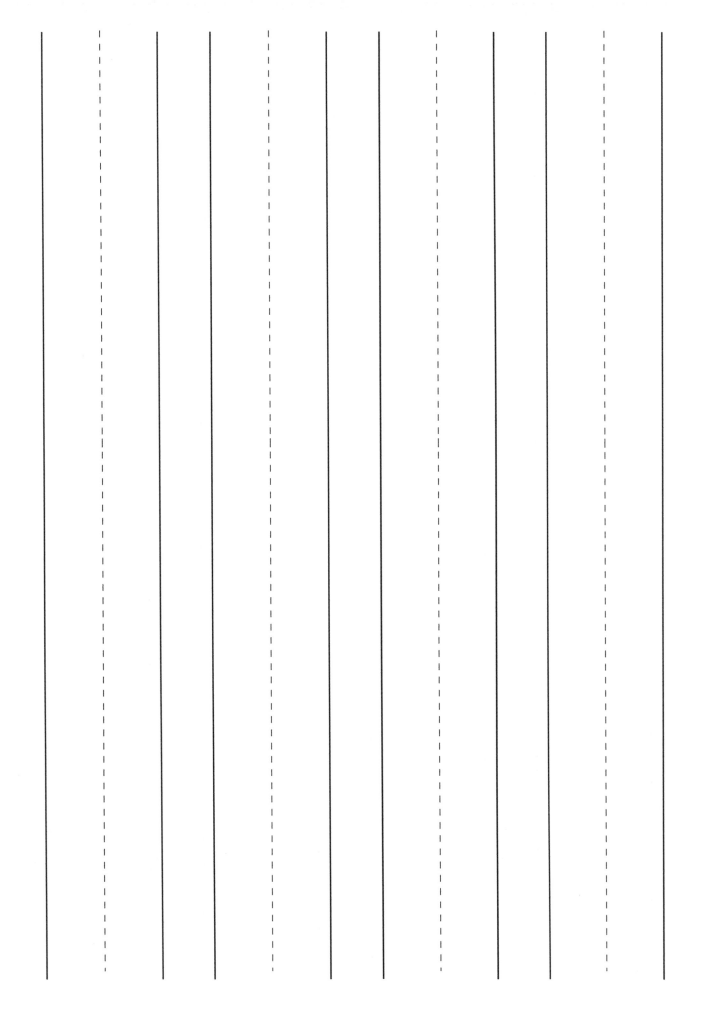

ABOUT ME

Thank you for purchasing this book! I hope you and your little one enjoyed doing all the activities together and that your child has a better understanding of letters and the sounds they make. Here's a little bit about me in case you were wondering who wrote this.

My name is Carli Smith, and I live in Utah with my hubby and two daughters. I have a Bachelor of Science degree in Special Education with an emphasis in Child and Family Studies. I taught Special Education for three years and assisted teachers with specialized testing for two years. I currently teach English classes online and get to spend the rest of the day with my girls! I love to read, be with my family, and eat treats.

If you have any questions or would like to contact me, please email me at: CarliSmithABC@gmail.com